DESIGNING & HOOKING PRIMITIVE RUGS

Susie Stephenson
Photographer Jay T. Stephenson

4880 Lower Valley Road, Atglen, Pennsylvania 19310

Published by Schiffer Publishing Ltd.
4880 Lower Valley Road
Atglen, PA 19310
Phone: (610) 593-1777; Fax: (610) 593-2002
E-mail: Info@schifferbooks.com

Library of Congress Control Number: 2009931038

All photographs are by Jay T. Stephenson unless otherwise noted.

Designed by Stephanie Daugherty
Type set in Grover Heavy/Humanst521 BT

ISBN: 978-0-7643-3288-3
Printed in China

DEDICATION

Welcome mat.

This book is dedicated to my mother, Joan Stephenson, who placed her hook in my hand and first taught me how to hook.

This book is also dedicated to my husband Tom, for his constant encouragement and my children David, Joseph, Maggie and Nathaniel for all their artwork and the fact that they don't mind the piles of wool, frequent stops at yard sales and wool soup for supper.

Special thanks go to Tom Blackford for so many things it is hard to list, Jessie A. Turbayne for writing the foreword, to my brother Jay T. Stephenson who took most of the photos in this book, and Reneé Post for putting up with the chaos of that week. Special thanks also to Tammy L. R. Meserve, Marion Brown, and Pam Van Siclen, for proofing the manuscript, and to Maggie Hoyt for helping with the typing.

Special thanks go to my grandmothers, Olive Ruby Stephenson and Eunice Cilley Brown, who taught me to knit, sew, embroider, and other forms of handwork.

All photos in this book are by Jay T. Stephenson unless otherwise noted.

FOREWORD

by Jessie A. Turbayne

A few years back I was addressing an audience of hooked rug enthusiasts at the Maine State Museum in the capital city of Augusta. The topic being discussed was hooked rugs and the pivotal role the Pine Tree State had played in the history and continuing tradition of the craft. When the lecture ended and the time came for questions my attention was diverted to a pretty young woman with blonde hair and an infectious smile who was wearing a hand-hooked coat of many colors. I cannot honestly remember her question but I do clearly recall walking away from the podium and into the audience after she offered to let me try on her unique work of art. The coat fit me perfectly and I know she was pleased. This hand-hooked fashion statement was the story telling canvas of a woman who obviously found much joy in its design and creation. In spite of the fact that she declined my offer to wear the coat home...she smiled...I smiled and thus began my growing interest in the hooked folk art of Susie Stephenson.

Jessie Turbayne is an internationally recognized authority on hooked rugs and the author of seven books that are highly regarded by both collectors and contemporary hooking artists.

TABLE OF CONTENTS

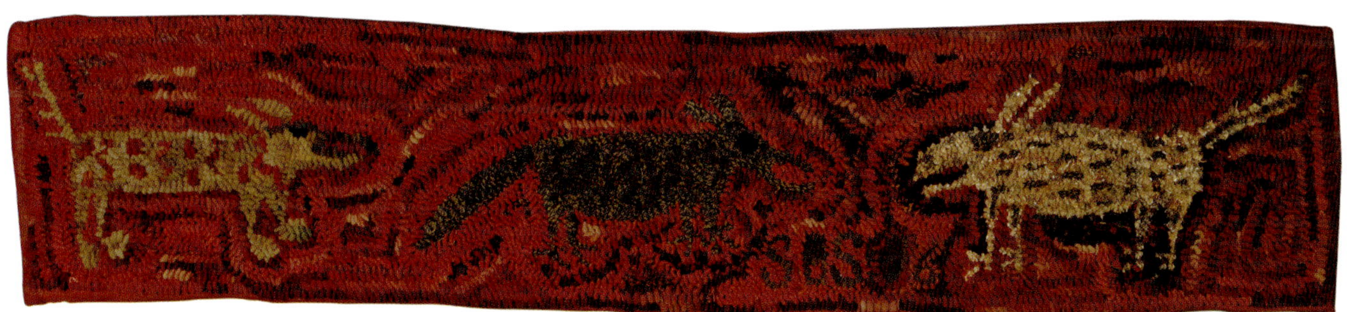

INTRODUCTION

I did not set out to become a hooker. It just kind of happened. Before I knew it, I went from having a hobby, to having a basket of wool, to a few projects on the go, and a few more I couldn't wait to start. All of a sudden, I realized I had bags, cupboards, shelves, and an entire room full of wool and rugs. It has invaded all aspects of my life, first in little ways, then it began to define me. It constantly surrounds me. People have begun to know who I am. My creations have been in galleries. Suddenly, I am turning the personal scrapbook of my work into an actual book. It is scary, exciting, and exhilarating, all at the same time. Oh well, it's the journey, right?

My mother taught me to hook when I was thirty. She taught me to do a lot of things for which I am grateful, but for teaching me to hook that hot week in the summer in Nova Scotia I will always be indebted to her. I drew out a little cat on a scrap of burlap and she placed her hook in my hand and taught me to pull up the loops. I finished that rug in a week and still have it. I came back to Maine, Tom built me a frame, and I continued to hook.

I love every aspect of hooking. I love the hunt for great wool at Frenchies, which is Goodwill, Canadian style. All the second hand shops around know me. I have a few favorite haunts that will save a few choice pieces for me. I love taking the garments apart and thinking of my grandmothers, how they remade clothing for their families, or sewed quilts for warmth. I think of my grandmothers each time I take apart a nice blazer and cut it up to recycle into a rug. I remember discussing quilting with my Grammie Brown one time, and she thought it was outrageous that people would buy new fabric, cut it into tiny pieces and then make patchwork out of it. She wouldn't have used a new piece of wool and neither would I! I enjoy drawing the design, dyeing the wool, and pulling up the loops.

When Grammie Brown died I helped my relatives clean out the farmhouse and took home the bags of cloth that she had left me. In one of the bureau drawers I found a dozen mittens, all singles, tied up with a piece of string. I had worn these mittens as a child. She had knit some of them at least, and darned more than a few to keep them serviceable. Obviously, she could not bear to throw them out and neither could I. I brought them home. They were priceless as jewels to me. I framed some of them. For many centuries, women's work hasn't been valued or looked at as art. I feel my rugs are art.

Even when you are "getting away from it all," hooking still follows you and is important in your life. Some years ago my husband and I set out for a much needed enchanted evening at a hotel not far from our home. We were away from all our four children at the same time. Dinner was included in the package, plus the pool and hot tub; we were very excited. We checked out the dining room after a swim and discovered that Tom needed a suit jacket to get into the restaurant. He hadn't brought one. I'm not sure if he even owned one at that time. We decided we'd go out for pizza and beer instead. So off we went to the shopping center and right beside the pizza place was a Goodwill store! In we went, giggling, as we picked out a five dollar jacket that was 100 percent wool and a great color that would look good in a rug. I don't think it fit very well. Anyway we went back to the room, got dressed up, and went down to the fancy restaurant. Tom took off the coat and hung it on the back of the chair and we proceeded to have a wonderful evening. I'm sure others in the restaurant were wondering why we were so happy!

When we got home, I washed it, dried it, and promptly cut it up and used it in Joseph's Sledding rug. Cast off clothing has found its way into many rugs, such as the red shirt I was wearing when Tom proposed to me, my Great-Aunt Lizzy's pants, Great-Aunt Rachel's blue skirt, and Grammie Brown's favorite Pendleton® suit. And, of course, a lot of other people's clothing too.

I never looked at clothing the same way again. I admire my friend's clothing and ask, "When you're done with that beautiful wool shirt may I have it for my rugs?" Later, when they are ready to throw it out, they give it to me and I recycle it into a rug.

My children don't wear wool like Tom and I do, nor do they draw pictures any more, but I continue to hook rugs. It is a passion with me. Ideas for rugs don't go away; they possess me and do not let go of me until I free them into a rug. Wool is my paint, the linen my canvas. I am a folk artist, untrained and uneducated in art, yet a deep need to create resides in me.

I hope you enjoy my rugs and their stories. I also hope they inspire you to create some rugs of your own.

Susie Stephenson
Edgecomb, Maine 2008

"My First Mat," 1994, 14" x 15". This is the very first rug I hooked. My mother told me to draw a simple picture on the burlap and then placed her hook in my hand. How many of us hookers can say our mothers taught us the craft? Hooking background became so boring I just put in a few flowers (primitive padullas). Notice how the cat is off centered. Author's collection.

BASICS OF HOOKING

The process of hooking has changed little over the last 150-200 years. A hook is used to pull thin strips of fabric through holes in a piece of backing, thus making loops. Many of these loops form a soft, low pile and usually the colors are changed to make a pattern or picture emerge on the top of the rug.

The basic equipment required for hooking has changed very little as well. You need a hook, a frame, a backing with a design drawn on it and some strips of wool. As with many crafts, it can become expensive if you buy preprinted patterns on linen, all new pre-dyed wool and use the biggest fastest cutters, not to mention frames, lights, and a fancy hook!

Natural light from the north side of the house is best, both for hooking and for color planning your rug. You might have to rearrange the room a bit so you have the best spot for hooking.

Wool rags were often used, as were other fabrics such as cottons, silks, and blends. These were ripped or cut into strips by hand or by using a simple machine and pulled through the backings of burlap or linen. I have hooked on burlap, monk's cloth, and primitive linen. I love the primitive linen best of all and hook exclusively on it now.

Backing materials can be very expensive or quite cheap, depending on their quality. The backing needs to have holes of sufficient size in it so the loops can be pulled through easily, but they should not be too big, as it is the friction of these loops on each other that holds them in place. These holes are formed from the warp and weft of the woven linen. In primitive linen they are bigger and open up when the hook is put into the backing. The whole backing needs to be stretched over the frame tightly. This makes it easier to pull the loops through. One can use a frame with gripper strips or carding strips similar to strong velcro® or the backing can be fastened to the frame with long tacks. In some older frames the backings were actually sewn into the frame. The advantages to using the carding strips are your rug can be moved around so you can hook whatever part you want, it goes on or off easily and it can be tightened quickly. These hooked strips can be accidently pulled out from the backing if the rug is pulled from the gripper strips in the wrong direction.

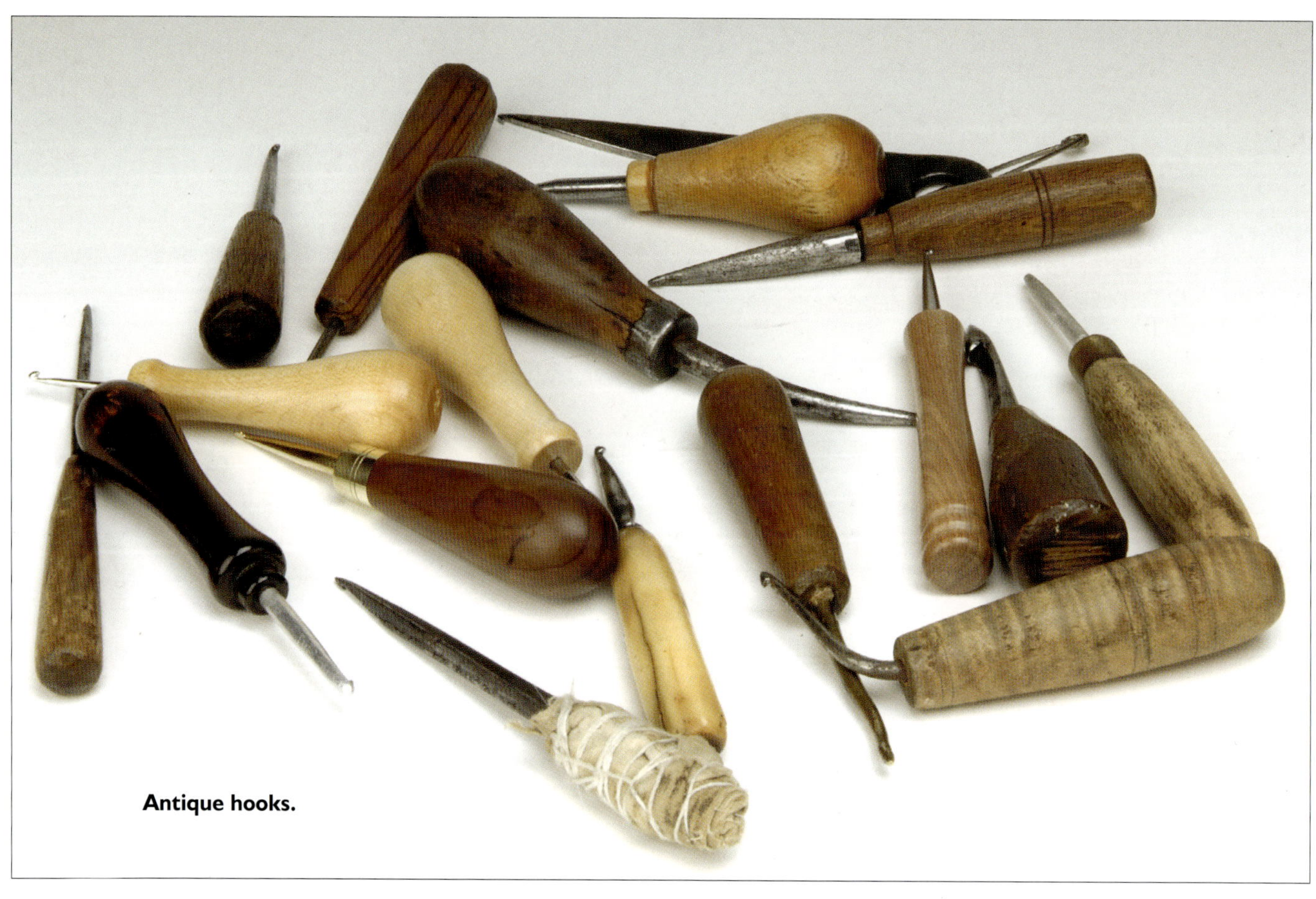

Antique hooks.

Favorite hooks.

This is a homemade frame my husband made with the gripper strips added.

Carding strips will eventually lose their grip. I have found that if you clean them regularly with a firm wire dog brush or carding comb, then vacuum them, they work as good as new. A friend gave me a simple little tool that cleans hairbrushes that works great for cleaning carding tools. A backing attached with tacks will rust and weaken your rug if it takes a long time for you to hook.

Round, heavy duty quilting hoops can serve as a frame as well. Make sure your screw is long enough to tightly hold your backing in place. A hardware store is a great place to find a screw long enough to convert a quilting hoop.

Old rug hooking frames and quilting racks have places to sew the backing right in. Some require C clamps in the corners to fasten it together and a chair at each corner to hold up the frame. Others have their own legs and can tilt. The twill tape for the edging was sewn directly onto the backing first (front and back) then this was sewn to the frame. It was then rolled so you worked from outer edge towards the center. When the hooking was finished, the rug would be taken from the frame and was ready for the floor. If your frame was large enough, more than one person could hook at a time. Sometimes people used pine picture frames to hook in. Some people don't use a frame at all.

After obtaining a suitable backing and frame, the next most important item will be the hook. There are many different ones to choose from. Hooks with small shanks are good for fine cuts and ones with large shanks are good for wide cuts. There are hooks with curved shanks, hooks like pencils, and old-fashioned wrought iron handmade hooks. Many shops will let you experiment with several until you find one you like. If you hook with a group you will see many different varieties of hooks. Hookers, being a friendly lot, will usually let you try their hooks so you can see if you like it and want to buy one. One of my favorites is an old hook from Prince Edward Island. It fits so nicely in my hand that it almost feels like the hook is hooking by itself, or that someone is standing over my shoulder and hooking my rug for me. I have other antique hooks that are little more than a ground off nail with a rag tied to the end. My other favorite hook is an Irish hook.

Like many hookers I know, I collect old hooks. I love the feel of old hooks in my hands and add to my collection whenever I can. I marvel at the ingenuity of some of the old timers who filed the shank to reuse an old broken fork or nail until it made a hook.

Once you find the one that is right for you, keep it safe, especially if it is an old one and therefore irreplaceable.

If you want to start off easily and inexpensively, a kit may be the ideal solution. Most kits come with the pattern drawn, the exact amount of precut wool needed, a hook, directions, and sometimes may include a frame. Kits are an inexpensive way to find out quickly if hooking is for you.

Designs can be drawn on easily with a black Sharpie®. I drew my first design and used my mother's scraps for the strips. Designing rugs is not for everyone, but maybe you can draw the design on yourself or have someone else do it for you. You can purchase one that someone has already printed or stenciled. If you choose to draw your own, use a permanent marker! If you make a mistake drawing, don't get discouraged, put lines through it and then draw the correct one. Or simply turn your backing over and start again. Sometimes different colored Sharpies® are not colorfast.

Sometimes the permanent markers go through the backing, marking the table, floor or tablecloth underneath. Place some newspapers down first! Whatever you decide, you are now on your way! If you designed your own you will want to zigzag a couple of rows around the edge of your backing material so your backing won't fray. Duct tape or wide masking tape work too, if you don't have a sewing machine handy. I find tape doesn't come off very well and leaves a sticky residue that has to be cut off.

This is a linen backing. Draw your design with permanent markers, but remember that sometimes the ink goes through the backing and onto the surface below. Place some newspapers down first.

Strips can be cut with scissors or by using one of a number of cutters with different blades the desired width. I cut exclusively using scissors or by tearing. Try to use 100 percent wool or at least 80 percent and up. Sometimes companies will put 100 percent wool on the labels when this is not so. Rip it! You can tell by the feel and the sound. I know it sounds crazy but it is true. Go find an old Pendleton® shirt or suit. It is 100 percent. Rip it and listen carefully. Also, when you dye something that is not wool sometimes some of the fibers don't dye. Cottons and linens wear okay in rugs, but they do not hold their colors. Check your labels and if something is a fantastic color and you only need a bit, then it is probably okay to use. I feel this makes my rugs look more primitive and much older. At one point in time I was given a box of precut strips. I did use them, but I was quite sick of hooking them when I was finally done with that box! I just couldn't bear to throw them away. You know, they were wool! Sometimes even now I'll find one in my box of scraps. Where do they all come from?

When cutting your wool to create a primitive, I find the best way to do it is to cut by hand or rip it. Scissors work great, but you have to stay straight on the grain of the fabric. You can cut any width you want, but some backgrounds work better with thin strips. I cut and rip my wool into many different widths. If your wool doesn't stay together when you are ripping it, you may be trying to rip it too narrow. Rip it wider, then cut down the middle and make two strips. For fine details like faces, use thinner strips. I love to hook with ripped wool because the edges are hairy. When the rug is pressed these mesh together and it looks more like an old rug, and the edges of the strips are less noticeable.

Cutting wool on a Rigby Model H cutter. A #8 cut creates strips 1/4-inch wide.

Ripping the strips of fabric.

The general rule of thumb is that you need four times the amount of wool as the area you want to cover with hooking. Fold your fabric twice to premeasure. If the linen area you want to hook is 2" x 2", you'll need wool that is at least 8" x 8".

Trying to figure out if you have enough wool to do a project can be a daunting task for a beginner. That is why kits are so popular. A good rule of thumb is four times the area to be hooked. Fold your piece of wool (before you cut it into strips) so it is four layers and place it over the area you want to hook. If it covers the area you are fine. I hook high so I allow 6 or 7 times the area. Sometimes I go shorthanded then pick another piece of wool that I think will work and attempt to blend it in. If I run out I very often do not have the recipe for dyeing more. I don't lose sleep over it, I just fill in with something similar.

Stretch the backing, design side up in your frame and tighten it. As I am right handed, these directions are for right-handed people. Holding your hook in your right hand, place it on top of your rug and frame, which should be on your lap if it's a lap frame. Place the strip in your left hand under the rug where you are to stick your hook into a hole and pull up the loop and the end. The second loop should be away from you to lock the first in place. Then holding the strip carefully in your thumb and index finger, follow where you will hook next, being careful not to twist the loop, put the hook through the linen and pull up. I pull the loop to the back a bit and this keeps the previous loop from getting pulled down under the backing. It is easier to hook toward you or in a straight line.

Hook around the outside of the figure with the first row of background to help it keep its shape, then fill in. If you are hooking a face, do the eyes and features first, then fill and do background. Hook a row around your figure before you hook the rest of the background. This helps it hold its shape too.

Hook in different directions and when you finish the length of wool, pull up the end. Through this same opening pull up your next loop and carry on. Later you can go back and trim the ends. You can pull up the end when you are finished with the color or when you don't want to go on with it.

Before I start to hook, I zigzag three times around the edge of the rug to prevent the backing from fraying. Twill tape is sewn to the edge.

Hooking the first row. When you finish a length of wool, pull up the end.

Outline whatever you are hooking first.

The current rule is to pull your loops as high as your strip is wide. I like to hook high because I like the way a new rug feels, kind of squishy to walk on. If you are hooking with different cuts, pick a medium height and try to follow that. Very soon in your hooking you establish the right height for you. I hook much higher than either of my sisters or my mother hook.

Later you can go back and trim the ends. Pull up and cut off.

Cut or rip your strips to the desired width. Small strips will give you more details. Wide strips are good for background. I like to use both.

Backgrounds can be hooked in straight lines, curves, squiggles, swirls, or whatever strikes your fancy. You don't have to hook every hole but don't leave large areas of backing showing on the front. Packing makes it so tight that your rug will kind of hump up. Sometimes steaming takes this out, sometimes not! The best way I have found to keep from packing is to think you are running out of wool!

Organizing Your Hooking

What I love about primitive hooking is that you have a lot of fabrics and textures at your disposal. When doing fine shading and very fine hooking you tend to use swatches of different values and hues, a color wheel, and a lot of other stuff that I know nothing about, never having had a formal fine shading hooking class in my life.

So why am I talking about it? This is why. When you buy swatches you cut each one as you use it, especially when doing a very thin, fine cut like an Oriental. You don't cut a lot of wool at a time nor do you have lots left. Primitive hookers tend to carry a lot of wool around with them because they might need it. Sometimes they change their minds about a color or want to add something different to a rug. They may not have their whole rug planned out precisely in advance!

A basket of random leftovers comes in handy for future projects that I didn't plan background on until too late.

Maybe there's a better way to do it, but I organize my wool according to the rug I am working on. In the beginning they are tied loosely together into bunches. Some people like zip lock bags but I find I don't like the plastic. These bundles are put in a basket or bag and left next to my frame and favorite chair. If your basket doesn't have a cover, expect your cat to be in it quickly. LL Bean® canvas totes work well too, especially the ones that zip it all together. I like these bags, especially if they have a small pocket to keep your hook and scissors in. After you have hooked for a while your wool gets undone from the bundles and mixed up. If I am hooking a rug and the entire background is an antique black, I will cut and rip my strips, put all these different strips into a large paper bag, then randomly pull out a strip and hook it. I do the same with my leftover strips of different colors when I am hooking a hit-or-miss background or border, or something that has many diamonds or circles in it. It is a fantastic way to use up my leftover strips from other pieces. This way you really don't get to pick an exact color and it provides a randomness to your rug that looks antique when it is finished.

After you have started hooking and are on your way to your second, third, or fourth project, you are well into the craft. You will find yourself looking differently at all the clothing in the family and asking yourself, "Will it hook and what will it look like hooked up?" You will start scouring the flea markets and thrift stores, especially on bag day.

Sort your wool by color. You decide if you want your plaids in with your solids or if you'd rather have them in a different container. I try to organize them on my shelves by color. Although my intentions are good, they soon become disorganized. I often have a problem of deciding where to put that beautiful plaid; in the greens or in the blues? As long as I can see a piece of it on the shelves, I know I have it and I will usually get around to using it.

After hooking a couple of rugs you will notice you have a lot of strips left over. Don't throw them away or save and label them, "Boat rug 2000." If that rug needs mending later on, are you really so organized that you will be able to pick that up? And if you are, will your rug be exactly the same color or will it be faded?

I started a boat bag, then a box with a cover for all those strips. It is handy for one or two strips of color for a cat's eye or something. They add up fast and if you don't find a project for them quickly, you will soon be overrun with them.

When my box is full, I know it is time to hook a rug using all my scraps or some small projects that don't require a lot. It's kind of like cleaning out a closet. It makes me feel virtuous. These rugs hook up quickly because all the strips are already cut and they have a free feeling to them. I think it's the hodgepodge of colors. It is fun to look at a rug and say "oh, that blue is Grammie's dress and it was the sky in the brick house rug or that yellow is the same as in the Tulip rug or Sam rug. Before hooking with this basket of strips, put them in the dryer to de-lint them.

Some great designs for using up these scraps are a border or background of multicolored stripes. A cat's paw or log cabin are other good traditional designs for this purpose (see geometric chapter). Actually, any geometric or small project is good for this. A farm scene with a lot of animals or people in it is another great way to use up your strips.

Color Planning Your Rug

I use this term loosely because on one of my first rugs (a cat's paw) I got all of the circles, both colored and black, hooked. I called my mom and asked her what I should use for the background. She replied, "Oh Susie, you should have decided that at the beginning!" I didn't rip out what I had hooked but chose a grey and hooked the background in. Some of my circles show up nicely and some are smaller and seem to fade into the background. I think it makes it look older.

Now I think in terms of lights and darks. Do I want a dark background or a light one? From there I pick two or three other colors to go with it. At least one should be a plaid or tweed. You might pick one a bit darker and one lighter or dye them that way by using the same water and dye, but taking them out every ten minutes to get a graduated color.

Pick out your colors and fabrics in daylight. You have a truer sense of the actual color that way. The new Ott® lights are supposed to give you wonderful true color. I don't own one but people who do swear by them. I still think it is better to pick out your fabrics and color plan your rug in daylight. Once when I was hooking at night, I went into my back room and got some black to use in a rug. I cut it and hooked it that night only to discover the next morning that it was navy blue, not black. I hate to pull out strips and do it over again!

Put all your wool for the project onto the backing. Then stand back and look at it with the lights on and off! Squinting also works or taking off your glasses and looking at it from afar. Usually, if a color is wrong you will see it! Beware of your greens. Choose between a blue green or a yellow green. Both will not look right together in your rug. (Another rule to be broken!) Someone once told me that nature doesn't follow that rule. Why should we?

Color planning: the colors are hooked as kayaks.

FINISHING TECHNIQUES

Simple Edges

I love to hook rugs, but dislike finishing off the edges. The way you finish off your rug may make the difference of whether it is around for the next generation or not.

Before I start to hook, I zigzag three times around the edge of the rug. I don't worry about thread color because on the finished product this will not show. One row is very close to the edge. One row is about an inch or inch and a half in from the edge. The next row curves a lot, almost zigzags so it touches both of lines. This holds the linen in place. Later on, when you are finished hooking you may need to sew another row closer.

Twill Tape

The easiest way to finish a rug off is to sew twill tape on the front side, press it, then turn it over and handstitch it onto the back. Make sure you wash it first, dry it, and press it. Always buy a few inches extra because cotton does shrink. Old time hookers left about a 1/4 inch of the tape on the front. This finishing technique may weaken your mat because it doesn't leave extra foundation around the edge that is covered with tape. The fibers of your foundation will pull and loosen up eventually causing a hole to start. Perhaps this way is okay for a wall hanging or a rug going onto a floor where there isn't a high amount of traffic.

Turned edge

This is a standard rug finish: a whipped edge with twill tape covering the folded linen edge.

Sometimes edges are just turned over (to the back), pressed and sewn tightly so the edge is caught. This will work if you have enough linen left around the edge and you haven't hooked too closely to the rug's edge. Linen is strong and it strengthens when wet. I think this way will wear fine, especially if you turn your rugs often and check the edges.

Whipped

At first, I whipped the edges over cording, using a wool that had many colors in it. It takes a long time to whip over and over but it really feels strong when you are done. My rugs that I have whipped have held their shape and have worn well even in high traffic areas. Tape is then sewn to the back to cover up the rows of stitching. I have also used a wide piece of wool for this. Sometimes, I use a color of tape or wool that coordinates with the rug. Sometimes, I have to fold the linen edge in a bit and then sew it down. I feel this is preferable to cutting it off.

Braided Edges

Sometimes I braid strips of wool and sew this to the outside of the rug . If it is an extra small rug, I try to make it larger with the braids. I think it strengthens the edge of the mat. The back edge where the braids meet the rug should be covered over with the twill tape or another wide piece of wool so it covers at least one braid. This neatens up the rug and strengthens the rug as well.

Tongues or Petals

Pieces of wool cut out in tongue shapes can be sewn around the edges. These should first have a piece of wool sewn around the edges that will be exposed. I cut out many tongues and cut strips on the bias so they stretch and curve nicely around the edge. I have a bunch of these ready to work on road trips and in waiting rooms. They are much easier to cart around than frames, rugs, strips, etc. I don't worry about colors because usually I dye them all together before I sew them onto my rug. Wool that is too thick for hooking, like old coats, works well for this. I have also finished the edges with a buttonhole stitche or a blanket stitch and a flower in each one. I have sewed one

A braided edge increases the size of a hooked rug, and strengthens it. The design for Othello was a trace of a wooden cutout my father made for me. I found a picture of an old weathervane in a book and we made the cutouts from that. Care needs to be taken while figuring out where to end the braid so it looks right. Braiding uses some of the thicker pieces of wool that are unsuitable for hooking. The braid also contained some of the colors or fabric that was actually in the main part of the rug. Collection of Tom and Joan Stephenson, East Jordan, Nova Scotia.

row of petals on and other times I have sewn three or four rows onto a rug.

If you have a particular rug for them to go on, maybe you'll want to size them perfectly. Say your rug is 24 by 18 inches. Petals can be any size you want but for this rug 2 or 3 inches would be the best because both 24 and 18 are divisible by 2 or 3. If you do it by two, 24 divided by 2 is 12. 18 divided by 2 is 9. Then add 12+12+9+9=42. For one row you would need 42 petals. Some people like to do an extra one at the corners so lay out your petals around your rug and take a look. You decide. You can make a few extras too, just in case you change your mind. Put them all in your dye pot with tea bags, onion skins, coffee or whatever color you decide, some laundry soap, and let them simmer away. Rinse and dry in the dryer, but don't let them dry all the way. Take them out of the dryer and press with a hot iron. A little moisture in them makes the steaming go quickly. Sew all these to the edge of the rug, then take a large piece of wool and sew the rug and all the petals to it. If you don't do this, the petals will rip and fall off. Mine got caught in a door.

Blanket stitches secure a three-tiered set of petals.

A double layer of petals was finished with edge strips before being attached to a rug.

Petals are especially good for a rug with a simple design. It livens it up and gives it a bit more character. On a busy rug they add too much stimulation and this makes the rug look fussy.

The Eaton Edge

I have a friend in Nova Scotia who designed this edge. Her name is Doris Eaton. Before she hooks her rugs she draws the design on and then does her stay stitching or rows of zigzag around the outer edge of her rug. Next she sews the binding tape or wool, whatever you prefer to use, to the line that represents the outer edge of your rug. Handsew the edge of your binding onto the front of your rug at that line. Turn your rug over and do one row of hooking very close to the edge of the sewn border so the rug design is turned over. This row of hooking becomes the cording. This color should

The first row is hooked next to the twill tape on the reverse side.

The rug is pressed through a wet dishcloth.

represent your border. Now hook your whole rug. The only thing left to do when you finish is to press it and trim the edge, then sew the binding tape down on the back. About a quarter of an inch of binding tape will show along your edge. The row of reverse hooking forms your cording and makes your edge a bit rounded. I believe this keeps your backing from folding in a sharp line and breaking off with wear.

Pressing

The last thing necessary to finish your rug is to press it. I do this both before I finish the edge and after I get the edge done. It can be done on the table or floor depending on the size of your rug. Place your rug on an old towel, wet a dishcloth, and place this on one part of your rug. Press down with a hot iron. Do not iron back and forth, but keep pressing over areas until your rug is finished.

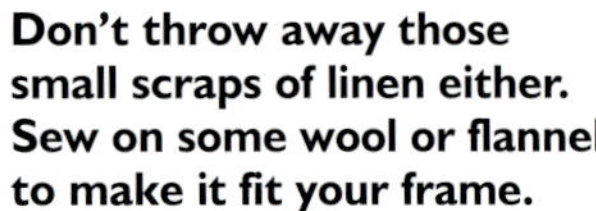

Don't throw away those small scraps of linen either. Sew on some wool or flannel to make it fit your frame.

DYEING WOOL

Lots of my wool I just wash and use as is. There are many wonderful commercial dyes for wool. Find one that works well for you. I use Majic carpet®, 3H Designs® and Cushing's *Perfection* Dyes® depending on my project, but my favorite dyeing methods are explained below.

I have a large and ever changing supply of recycled wool pieces. They vary in size and weight. They are all washed, dried, and ready to cut or over-dye. Many are textures, tweeds, and plaids. Frequently the best textured wool comes from men's suit jackets. They are miserable to take apart, but there is nothing comparable to them for textures and interest when they are hooked. They make awesome animals.

Don't be scared to dye! It is fun and exciting and if something doesn't come out to your liking the first time, put it away for another rug. (Hide it at the bottom of the pile and maybe, when you find it again, you'll like it!)

If you want precise and never fail recipes for colors, go buy yourself a different book. This is for the relaxed, happy-go-luckies who like to experiment and have a good time doing it. I hook exclusively with old clothes or scraps of cloth from sewing reproduction Eighteenth Century clothing. I don't have a lot of money tied up in "white" wool or wool pre-dyed by other rug hookers, so I am really relaxed when it comes to dyeing. It is a surprise every time you dye something.

Save tea bags, coffee, onion skins, beet juice, or beet skins. Anything that stains your teeth or clothes will dye your wool. If you're worried about tea bags molding before you need to dye something, save them in plastic ice cream containers in the freezer. Tea bags and coffee grounds make a mud color darker if you leave them in for a long time and don't dye a lot of wool at once. Throw water and grounds in the garden or compost when you are finished dyeing!

Use as is wool or dye with onion skins, beet juice, and salt, or vinegar. Use simple, ordinary ingredients or spices and herbs that are readily available in most kitchens. I like this rule and follow it almost 100 percent of the time because often when I am hooking a rug, I think of times when people wanted a color but had no dyes so they made do with what was readily available.

Koolaid® also dyes well. I have a sensitive nose and can smell it for a long time afterwards so I don't use it.

I also dye wool over my fireplace. I have a large iron pot and I save my tea bags for a week, then add a lot of water and steep this over the fire. While this is happening, I pick out my pieces to dye. These are then soaked in soap and water. Laundry soap works fine for this, but other soaps also work, such as hand soap, dish soaps, and shampoos. The wool can soak for a few minutes to several hours to open up the fibers and make them ready to receive the color. When you think it has soaked long enough, put the pieces into the iron pot with the "Tea." You can put all the tea bags in a mesh orange or lemon bag. They are easier to remove that way and it creates an even tone for all the cloth to take up the dye. It also helps if you don't crowd your wool into the pot but make sure it can be easily stirred around.

I like my wool all mottled so I leave my tea bags in, crowd my wool, and don't stir a lot! Add 1 to 2 cups of vinegar or 1/2 cup pickling salt and simmer. These act

Dyeing wool over an open fireplace.

A close-up shows wool stewing in an iron pot.

as a mordant to set the color. Don't boil, it weakens the fibers in the wool and if you use them, that area will wear out quickly! Boiling also thickens or fulls the wool and it will be too thick to hook. When your wool is a bit darker than what you want (remember it is darker when it is wet) take it off the fire and let it cool. I rinse it again and again in the sink with warm to cool water until the water runs clear. I like to hang it out to dry but it can be spun in the washing machine and dried in the dryer.

Use an iron pot. You can pick up one cheaply at a flea market or yard sale. Probably you've got a relative that has one who'd be willing to give it away. I think the iron acts as a mordant (this sets the dye) too, but I still use vinegar or salt to be on the safe side. Sometimes when you dye with iron and it gets very hot, the wool can feel very harsh afterwards, so proceed with caution.

Don't use your dye pot for anything else. If you over dye wool, the soap pulls the color dye from the other wools and marries them together. I think we need to be cautious of this interaction of old dyes.

I carved a stirrer, a stick that looks like a Y. It has a bittersweet vine curved around it. I also have the one that belonged to my great-grandmother. Find one that works for you. It might take a while. An old wooden spoon works too. You might have to make your own or have your kids make it. You can always contact me and my kids will make you one for a donation. Secondhand shops and flea markets are great places to find old large wooden spoons and pots. I find that pasta tongs are great for picking pieces of wool out of the pot when it has picked up just enough color.

Set the wool color with a variety of mordants. Salt and vinegar are common ones. So is citric acid, the first ingredient in Koolaid®. Other ones that work but change the brightness etc. are iron, copper pennies, rusty nails, and alum. Don't be scared to experiment. You will find one that is right for you. I use a cup of vinegar per two gallons or about 1/2 cup of salt. If you are dyeing with beets and beet juice, use an enamel pan when you want a pinkish color. I learned this the hard way. One time I used my iron pot and let my juice soak for a day. When I got it hot I noticed the foam on the top was a beautiful pink. I thought it would get a deeper pink if I left it, but the next time I went to stir it, it was a beautiful warm brown. I soaked my pieces of wool and added them and then the vinegar. I simmered them for half an hour and let them cool down. They were a beautiful warm brown color. Not the pink I had intended, but beautiful nonetheless.

Marrying Colors

This is the easiest dyeing method and the one I use the most often to get great colors that look good in a rug together. Wool of different intensities and tones can be made to fit together in a rug by "marrying them." In this process, the colors of the various pieces are released, blended together, absorbed by the wool, and then set. Each piece now has something in common with the others.

Soak the wool for at least a half hour, and up to a day or so in warm water and soap (laundry soap, dish soap, or shampoo all work). Then heat the soaked wool, the water, and the soap in your pan on medium and watch to make sure it does not boil. When you think enough color has come out, add the vinegar and let it simmer another 1/2 hour. Sometimes, if not a lot of color comes out, you can add a couple of teaspoons of baking soda and this will release the colors. Let this all cool down, then rinse. You can do this in the sink with hot water, then gradually get cooler, but don't shock the wool with cold right away or you will felt it and your wool will be too thick to hook with. I dye large quantities and cram my pots full, so I rinse and spin in the washing machine then put it in the dryer. Sometimes, when it comes out, there are still a couple of colors that aren't right or some that thickened up too much. Don't use these!

Antique Black

I'm not sure why this is called antique black because it isn't really black, but blues, reds, purples, and greens married together. It is a variety of colors that blend well and, when seen together in a background, look dark, but really they don't need to have any black in them. To make antique black, put some dark wool in to soak with soap. Heat it up on medium. If you want to get colors that are more uniform, then leave lots of room in the pot. If you desire a lot of color change in one piece of wool, then crowd your wool into the pot. The heat and soap causes the color to bleed out of the wools. This turns the water muddy. Stir often, add the vinegar or salt and the wool pieces will pick up and absorb the colors. These colors will look great together in an animal or in a background. If you use all recycled wools like I do, then you will soon find that you have a lot more dark wools than lighter ones. This makes it easy to hook a lot of backgrounds in antique black because you always seem to have plenty around.

Most black or navy wool from woolen mills is over dyed. Sometimes they just look too harsh. I have found that these colors can be softened by soaking the wool in laundry detergent, heating it up in your pot and putting in either a little baking soda or ammonia. (NOT BOTH!) I use a teaspoon of baking soda because I hate the smell of the ammonia!

More Natural Dyes to Try

Spices, especially the dark ones, dye beautiful warm colors. I've used paprika, turmeric, and chili powder. I bought a box of spices at a junk shop and used some for making soaps. They sat around for a while longer and then I used them for dyeing. They smell good too! I figure that is an added bonus. I got out an old cream-colored blanket that I've hooked as is, but for dyeing I cut it into uniform, 9- x 18-inch sizes. I used four cups of water, a teaspoon of spice, and a tablespoon of vinegar and dyed them one at a time so I could really see the results. Amazing! I presoaked the wool, brought the water and spices to a boil, added the wool, simmered for fifteen minutes or so, added the vinegar and simmered for a half hour more. I let them soak for a while and cool down. This is the hardest part because you can't wait to see the results. The spices don't dissolve completely in the water and they do not all get absorbed either. I found that the wool then needs to be washed again because little bits of spice stay on the cloth otherwise. A spin in the dryer helps too! Maybe I just used too much spice. I did get some fantastic colors and have used this method repeatedly with good results. Different soaps change the colors and, of course, fresher spices do too! Remember, relax and have fun!

An example of antique black.

HOOKING HINTS

Save wool sweaters. These can be dyed before or after cutting. Cut from the waist to the shoulder in 1/2 to 3/4 inch strips, then pull to make sure they don't break. If they do, cut them thicker. They kind of curl up when you pull them. I find that putting some of these strips into a rug gives it a different texture. They can be used for one part, in particular, such as a tree, wall, or bush, or you can hook them throughout your rug.

Save socks and long underwear too. Again, these add texture and interest to your rugs. Beware of cottons, they do not hold their colors as well as wool, nor do they wear as well. If you are hooking a wall hanging this shouldn't be a problem.

Shop at secondhand shops on bag day and tell your friends that when they are cleaning their closets to remember you and your hooking. You'd be surprised at the gems you get.

If your sweater is too thick to cut into strips, unravel it and roll the yarn into balls. This makes nice sky and clouds. If you want to over dye it, unroll it and coil it like a rope. Tie every four inches or so, then put this in the dye pot.

I wash the items found at flea markets and thrift stores, or given to me by friends and store them. I don't take them apart right away. I wait. When I want to use one, I cut off an arm or leg or back and don't process or dye too much at a time.

Don't store wool in plastic. It makes it sweat, causing the wool to weaken. I have mine on shelves, in boxes or in canvas bags. This allows it to breathe. The rugs I am not using I roll, hooking out, and store inside cotton pillowcases.

Every piece of wool I bring into my house gets washed. I take no chances with moths! If it is a thicker piece, wash in cool water. If it needs to be fulled (thickened) a little, I wash it in warm. Dry as much as you can on the line. You don't ruin as much that way.

Organize your hooking into some kind of a system NOW! My wool room is such a mess right now that I can hardly find a special color, just like my desk used to be when I taught school! If organizing wool isn't your strong point, find someone to help you set up a system before it gets to be a monster of a job!

I have two large bookcases and each shelf is designated to a color. Once the wool is washed you can roll up the garment and store it that way or take it apart. Wool that has been taken apart takes up less space. It is much easier to find and pick a color that is appropriate for your rug if you can actually see what you have! If you decide to take apart the garment, save the tag and the waistband or collar to roll it up with. This also keeps the label with the wool so you'll know what you have, which is useful if you haven't mastered the rip wool test. Less than 100

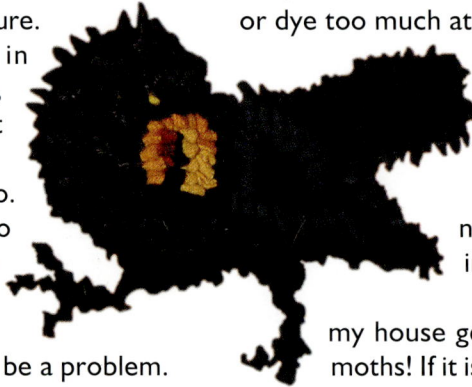

"Bill the Cat."

percent wool dulls your cutter blades or scissors and you'll need to sharpen them more frequently.

When the weather turns cooler and I begin to spend more time indoors I start to hook again. I never really stop in the summer, but I do not hook every day like I do from October to the end of May.

October tends to be my FIFI month (Find it and Finish it !) It is a great way to clean out, organize, and see what you've forgotten about or what needs to be finished.

There will always be ideas and inspirations for rugs. It is hard to try to keep up with them. Keep a notebook for sketches and little drawings. Maybe I should hook smaller rugs. NAH! Keep a record of your rugs and the inspiration for them. It is really entertaining to read and it will someday be a wonderful record of your rugs.

Sometimes rugs are designed around a beautiful piece of wool. Sometimes a Pendleton® bathrobe or shirt screams, "I will make a great background. Keep me for that!"

I buy all the Harris Tweed® jackets and coats I can find. They are hard to take apart but the texture they add to a rug is worth the time it takes. Sometimes the weave doesn't firm or felt up enough when you are washing and drying it. If this happens handcut it or rip the wool into large strips and cut down the middle. If the wool is too fragile to hook or it comes apart when you try to pull up the loop, your strip is too thin. Cutting it wider by hand should solve this problem.

When you are doing lettering and it doesn't show up enough, make sure you hook the area around it then pull the lettering out and hook it again. This really helps accent the lettering and it shows up much better. Don't use knits, if you can help it, to do the letters with. They blossom out more than the wool in different directions and cause the letters not to be crisp and the angles are blurred. Letters look much better when done with strips of a solid color and with regular wool.

As a young teenager, I started a collection of antique flat backed cookie cutters because I loved to bake. Antique, flat-backed cookie cutters create great template shapes for hooked rugs. I photocopy them and then used the shapes on my rugs. The little chicken is a special favorite. I use it when I make molasses and sugar cookies. It is so cute that I just keep using it.

This is a tracing of one of the old flat-backed cookie cutters that I bought at an antique show.

"Two Chicks," 2006, 36" x 21". The chickens were outlined in red and hooked with Kansas City Bronze formula, Cushing Dyes® (1 tsp. bronze, 3/4 tsp. med. brown, and 2 tsp. nugget gold for half yard of wool). The background was dyed with onionskins and is really quite a wide variety of light and dark fabrics. Artist's collection.

"Susie's Chickens," 38" x 21". My parents were visiting at my house and my mom decided to hook a rug just like the one I was hooking. So we traced the chickens on it any old way and started hooking. I got ahead and my kids were excited that it was a race. They became upset when she jokingly told them she was going to pull all mine out when I was at school teaching. Author's collection.

This is my mom's rug, made at the same time. I cannot remember who won, only that my kids were rooting for me! We whipped the edges before we sewed the petals on. Mine has an extra petal in each corner. Collection of Joan Stephenson, Port Joli, Nova Scotia.

DESIGNING PRIMITIVE RUGS

Rules to Hook By, or Not!

Simple Designs

What I find works the best is to use a child's picture and transfer it as best you can onto the linen. Having children draw directly onto the linen makes for a very interesting, complicated design because kids don't always use the same scale. Think differently. Think like a child. Think outside the box. Start with a new notebook and box of crayons, they are delightful. Use your non-dominate hand to draw the picture. Try to draw freehand and not use a straight edge. Use a fat marker and giant paper. Don't use an eraser or whiteout, just close your eyes and draw. Draw from memory. Use paints or a fat paintbrush or marker. How many lines does it really take to get the essence of the thing on paper? Keep your marker on the paper or linen and don't let up. Get on your belly on the floor and draw. Laugh! Don't take yourself too seriously! Get yourself some new markers, crayons, or paint and a lot of paper, and some kids to help you, your own or borrowed. Start drawing now. You're sure to get something wonderful out of that day. If not a lot of rugs, then a lot of new friends and cool artwork! Maybe you want to make the eye too big or place it off a little or make the whole head too big. I like to hook my chickens with both beaks and smiles.

Templates work for designing rugs. Be careful when you transfer them or your rug will be so precise that it will turn out looking not quite right. Kids and cardboard make great templates. If you don't have a budding artist around, maybe a friend or a grandchild can help you.

A child's drawing captures a purity of form perfect for a primitive rug.

INSPIRATIONS

As an elementary teacher, I always told my students, "Write about what you know!" It is the same with art: draw and hook what you know, what is around you, animals, pets, houses, flowers, and other pleasing designs and colors from your surroundings. They should all serve as inspirations for mats. I always hook water and boats when I am in Nova Scotia.

Another brief thought on color. I usually hook the colors of the seasons when I am hooking a rug. My autumn colors are always hooked in the fall, summers are for boats, water, and mermaids. In the deep dark of winter when I used to hook dark grays and blacks, I now make myself hook bright colors to get me out of my seasonal depression and through the winter months.

Keep your eyes open, design ideas come from interesting sources. Look around you at your seemingly ordinary life. Look for something special or unique about it. Look back into your childhood to favorite times or animals or houses. Hook memories. Nothing will be exactly perfect, but your rug will feel right. If you want a perfect replica or memory, take a picture. Children's drawings are a fantastic place to start. They are unhindered by the fact that their drawings are not perfect. Yet in their eyes they are. They have innocence about them, a charm that old rugs have as well.

I think the most important thing of all to remember is to relax and have fun. Rug hooking shouldn't be stressful. It should be enjoyable. It is a forgiving craft with as many or as few rules as you wish to adhere to.

When designing your own rugs there are a few things to consider. Do you want to have a large center subject like a cat or dog? Probably you will need to use a photo copier to enlarge the original artwork if you feel apprehensive about drawing it freehand onto the linen backing.

Decide if you want this subject hooked dark or light. This is relative because your subject will probably be

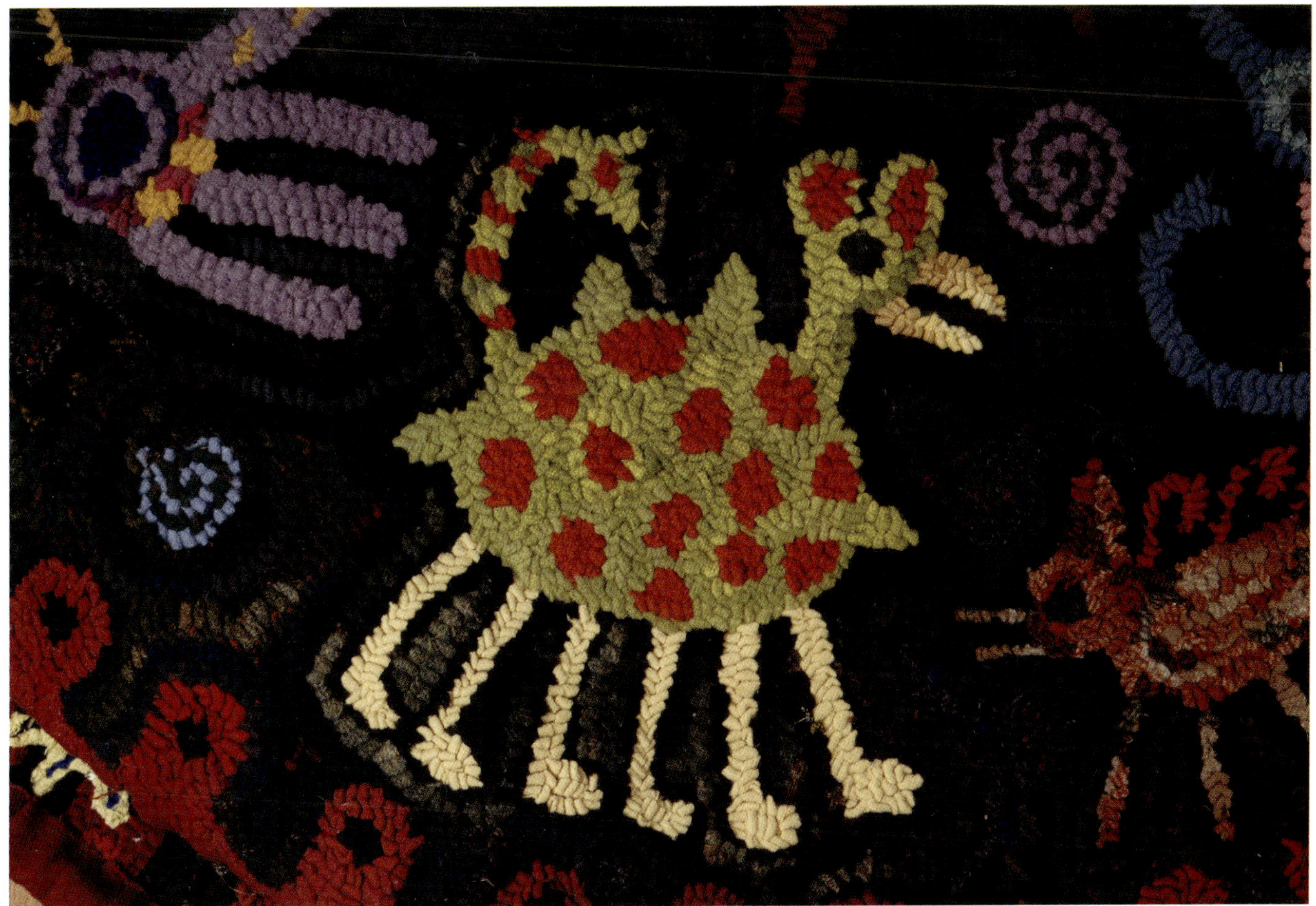

Children imagine fantastic creatures that adult minds can rarely create.

many colors or shades of one color, even if you are doing a primitive. If the subject is done out of the same fabric it can be boring. Plain wool can be flat and uninteresting unless it is put with other, textured wool.

Usually your background will be the opposite of your subject. This means that if your subject is dark you'll want to use a light wool for the background. You can also put a row of a different color to separate the subject from the background. Many old rugs use a dark black or sometimes a purple for this line. This can be done to separate the border from the background too. Some of the same colors can be used in both the subject and the background as long as they are not too close together in the rug.

Backgrounds can be mixed up colors, squiggles, circles, or whatever strikes your fancy. You can use black or tans, but as always, never use just one piece. Use a lot of different colors, marrying them so there are varied shades of brown or black. Sometimes my antique black has very colorful purples, blues, greens, and reds in it. I like a border, but that is just my preference. Do what you want or let the size of your linen background determine that.

I keep a file folder with kid's sketches or photos of things that might make good subjects for rugs. I have a folder in my file cabinet and when I need an idea, I pick one. Usually something more pressing comes up and the pictures just stay in my file while another sketch gets made into a rug. Once the rug is finished, the inspirational picture or photo, along with a picture of the finished rug and the stories behind it go into my scrapbook. I am trying always to get more organized or come up with a better system that works for me!

Negative space is a term that is relatively new to me and I use it when planning a rug. It is a place or places on your rug that allow the eye to rest. I liken this to a song that has a chorus or the notes that are within easy range, not very high or very low. These areas make the song interesting and exciting, but the chorus and the comfortable notes allow you to relax.

Lots of my rugs don't have much negative space or background in them. I am all about the subject and things relating to it, not the boring background. If your background is many tones of the same or similar colors, it will not be boring or overly exciting, but interesting. Also you won't get bored hooking it or decide to put something else in your rug because you are sick of hooking background.

Poison colors. These are the colors that make you squirm. They are perhaps a little garish or even somewhat exciting. Purple is a good one as well as fuchsia, orange, and lime greens. There are lots of other ones too. These create interest and excitement in your rugs. They should be used sparingly, perhaps in an eye, for whiskers, in a bathing suit or as the outline of an animal or at the center of a flower.

Will you have a border? Will it be thin or fat? If you have one, hook it in an uneven number of rows. Add an accent color or row if you want. You could also hook it so it looks like a frame. If your border is fat you might want to add a design into it or into the corners. Triangles in borders are fun, as are stripes, designs, or other motifs related to your rug. Borders don't have to be the same size on all sides. Our eye manages to compensate, when we see the rug, but often if you count the rows, old, primitive, hand-drawn rugs had uneven borders.

Do you want a design in the corners of your rug just inside the border? Flowers, posies, or primitive flower of some sort? Mice around a cat? The Max rug has a border with uneven edges and a large red dot in each part. The fox also has corner designs, chickens, and a feather.

Don't hook with a really stark white in a rug. Dull it down by overdying it or marrying it with other colors you're using. A quick bath in a cup of tea will change it just enough, unless you like your tea strong, like all the Nova Scotians I know! A little will go a long way! If you decide not to follow this suggestion your whites will jump out and glare at you! If in doubt, hook some white in and then squint at it. If it glares at you, use a different color white.

Another idea I love to use is when you don't know what color to use in a portion of your rug use purple. When in doubt, reach for the purples. I use a lot of purple and blues in my rugs. Sometimes it is very purple almost violet, other times it is barely colored at all. Purple is a magic color in a rug and I love to use it.

If you decide to design your own rugs, you get to pick out the design, colors, and cut your strips to whatever width you want. You are expressing yourself way before you start hooking. You can be as daring as you want to be or as safe!

If you decide to hook a pre-printed pattern, you can express yourself in your choice of the strip size, the colors to a certain degree, the height of your loops, and the direction of your hooking. A rug can look very different hooked in straight lines than when hooked in swirls and wiggles!

Hang your rug up or have someone hold it up for you so you can study it from afar. Usually if something needs to be changed, it jumps out at you from a distance. Sometimes you lose something into the background. Outline it with a darker color or a color with more contrast, like a poison.

If your background is many shades of one color use the lightest or the darkest to outline your figures. This makes them stand out more. You can also outline the figures with one or two rows of the background following the contours of the figure, then hook the background in a different direction.

Date and sign it always. I know you want it to look old but someday you will be trying to put the rugs you hooked in order and having them dated and signed really helps! Also, you can see how you develop as a hooker, early work and then later pieces. My mother hooks too and she signs her rugs like a friend of hers did, Ruth Twombly of Brunswick, Maine. She embroiders her name on the twill tape and sews it to the back. You can add your initials right into the rug where they will show, or hook your whole name bold! Hide your initials in the trees, in chimney smoke, in the waves, in the background, or in the border. Be creative.

Don't be sloppy or hook carelessly, but don't worry either. Primitives are not precise and that is part of their charm. Pressing with a damp cloth and a hot iron can even out a lot!

Don't be afraid to try new colors, but remember a little poison goes a long way. Try a different fabric other than wool, but be careful because if your rug goes onto the floor; the new, different fabric you used may be stronger than your backing and could rub when it is walked on and can break the fibers in your foundation. You will lose your rug or have to repair it. Using different fibers will work fine if you are making a wall hanging or if you plan to frame your finished project.

Ideas for borders.

Have fun and don't take it too seriously. Hooking should be pleasurable, like playing or drawing was when you were a child. If you run out of a specific kind or color of wool and you are doing a primitive piece you can do what old timers did, just hook the next little bit with another color, or dye more. If you have hooked with a variety of wools it shouldn't make much difference. Or you can pull out a few strands from somewhere else and hook them in, and then add another color. I like my backgrounds hooked with swirls and lots of colors, other folks like them straight across and flat so the flowers stand out. I always use some textured fabrics. I find this creates an illusion, making my animals move and my backgrounds sway.

DESIGNING RUGS USING A CHILD'S DRAWING

Children's drawings make wonderful primitive rugs. Think for a moment what it would be like to see the world through a child's eyes. We can't really do this but we can put those drawings that are in fact the essence of youth and innocence onto a rug and capture that exact moment forever. An entire book could be devoted to the different ways of doing this. It is amazing that, with a crayon or pencil, a blank piece of space (paper, boxes, chalkboard, or wall), and a few minutes of time, a child can create an animal that has so much character. Small children have a wonderful sense of animals; some have two legs, some four, some have wings, and most have two eyes. They may not pay much attention to exactly where they go! Hooking a rug is a wonderful way to make sure your child's artwork lasts for a very long time.

Keep a photo of the artwork nearby so you can consult with it to get it as exact as you need to. Since I never throw anything away we still have the painting of my son Joe sledding. It is dog eared and torn but we also have it preserved forever on a rug beside his bed.

I like to put my initials and the child's somewhere in the background. Often I just put in their whole name. I date it too.

Barbara Johnson, one of America's well known folk art collectors, has quite a collection of hooked rugs. She has one that is a collection of animals, leaves, flowers, and hearts. I based my idea of the menagerie on that hooked rug. I wanted to use the idea while also using my children's artwork for the rug. Mine turned out very different from hers.

When my kids were little they were always drawing. Like my father, I find it difficult to part with things, such as papers and drawings. I decided to put them on a rug, all helter skelter so there would be no right or wrong to the rug, making it look interesting from all angles and directions.

I'm going to give you some simple ideas that work for me when I am designing a rug from a child's drawing.

"Joseph Sledding Down the Hill," 1995, 32" x 23". One of the first rugs I hooked was designed by my son, Joseph. He brought home this drawing of himself sliding down a hill in kindergarten. There was a large tree that you just knew he would run into. He had painted it with a large brush and had painted outside of the lines. You could see the movement in the paint. When I hooked this piece I tried to hook it exactly this way. I also looked at a lot of snow that year and discovered that it was not only white but pink, purple, and blue as well.

"Bill," 2001, 14" x 18". Nathaniel, my youngest son, was seven when he drew this rug on a tiny box lid. I photocopied it and promptly put it on a rug. I tried to make the rug more useful, making it bigger by braiding an edge around it. I like the plaid texture of the background. Collection of Tom Blackford.

Sketch of Bill.

Sometimes the drawings just need to be copied onto the backing. Copy your child's artwork on a photocopier. Enlarge if necessary. Glue or instant adhesive these cut-out photocopies onto a piece of cardboard. Cut around. Then place on the backing and trace around. This makes a very sturdy template that can be used again. It is also great to be able to move it around on your linen to see exactly where it should go. You can also flip it over to get the reverse. This is especially useful when doing two cats that are facing each other. You can embellish this design by adding flowers to the corners or add something into the rug or border that will relate to the central piece of artwork.

You can also trace the photocopy onto the linen by taping the picture and then the linen onto a large window and tracing it. I have a friend that has a light table at work and she loves to transfer patterns of her grandchildren's work to rugs. I usually just draw it on freehand and it turns out close enough.

Another way to transfer your child's artwork is with an overhead projector. Take the drawing, transfer to an overhead transparency, and then project onto a wall, the desired length away, to make the rug the size you want. The backing can be taped or tacked to the wall and drawn directly on. Or this can be transferred to a large piece of poster board or paper and the templates can be made then. Make sure the whole design is traced at one time because sometimes projectors get moved and they are difficult to get back into exactly the same place.

Your child could also draw directly onto the linen. Draw your borders first or children will go right to the very edge!

Joseph Hoyt
to mom
this is me
riding a
horse

"This is me riding my horse!" 1995, 13" x 14". This is artwork by Joe. He was in grade one when he drew this. This rug makes you smile. The person doesn't have arms and I think the horse looks like a cat! Author's collection.

"Nat's Cat," 2000, 25" x 18". My son, Nathaniel, came home from school one day with this drawing. The school cat, Fessic, was missing. Nat thought his drawing would make a good rug. I added the padullas (primitive flowers) in the corners to pull out the colors on the cat's nose and mouth and tie them in with the border. Collection of Nathaniel S. Blackford, Edgecomb, Maine.

"Nat's World," 1995, 53" x 33". My children drew directly onto the backing, thus some animals are not to scale. My wool supply was small and I needed more greens. I'd buy another skirt and hook it. I drew more animals so I could hook less background. Because both the moon and sun were in the rug, I made some of the rug daytime with farm animals and some night with nocturnal ones. Collection of Nathaniel Blackford, Edgecomb, Maine.

"The Menagerie," 2004, 90" x 43". In this large rug, Menagerie, look closely at all the animals, especially the cow. Have you ever seen an udder like that? Yet, you know it's a cow. How can that pig stand up with all his legs there? How about the eyes in the redbird? In this rug we traced our hands. Mostly I enlarged and sometimes reduced drawings to fill up the spaces. These pictures were saved for quite a while because they just weren't right for a rug of their own. I told my children I couldn't keep up with making rugs for each of their drawings, but I would put them all together on a big rug. This large rug took me four years to hook. I got sick of hooking the antique black background and would put in more designs, like the four leaf clover or another animal. Author's collection.

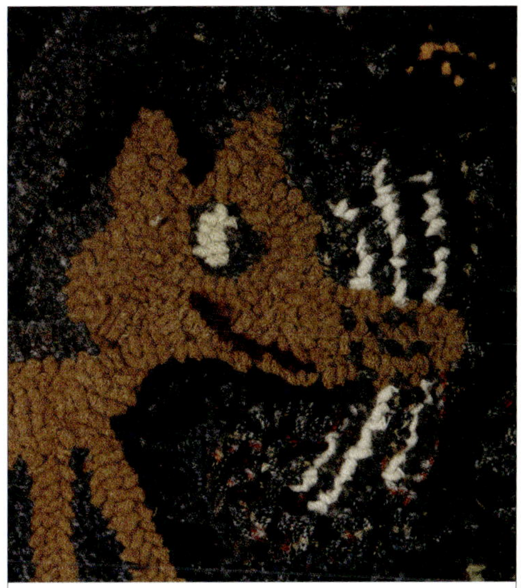

"The Fox," 2001, 20" x 18". For years I have kept chickens. In my grade three classroom we hatched eggs and also got day old chicks. We built a chicken house, fed them, tried to fence them in, chased them, loved them, and of course enjoyed their eggs. One year we had a lot of trouble with a fox. He would come get a chicken or two every few days. I was lamenting the loss of the chickens with my son, Nat, and he drew me the picture of the fox looking so crafty and pleased about his easy meals. The feather in that corner represents the chickens he got. Nat wrote The Fox right on the linen and I hooked it as he had printed it. Collection of Kathleen Mack, Round Pond, Maine.

"The Kittens," 2001, 18" x 14". Nat drew this rug right onto the tiny piece of linen. The background was hooked with a fluffy wool blanket, dyed with onionskins. The border was a large, checkered piece. I hooked it with one of the strips, not both. Notice both Nathaniel's initials and mine in the background. Author's collection.

"The Kayaking Race," 16" x 39". Joe did this drawing. When I designed the rug, I created templates of the kayaks and paddles on a separate piece of paper so I could move them around until I liked it. The great thing about the templates is you can use them again on a different rug or to make another pattern. Collection of Joseph Hoyt, Edgecomb, Maine.

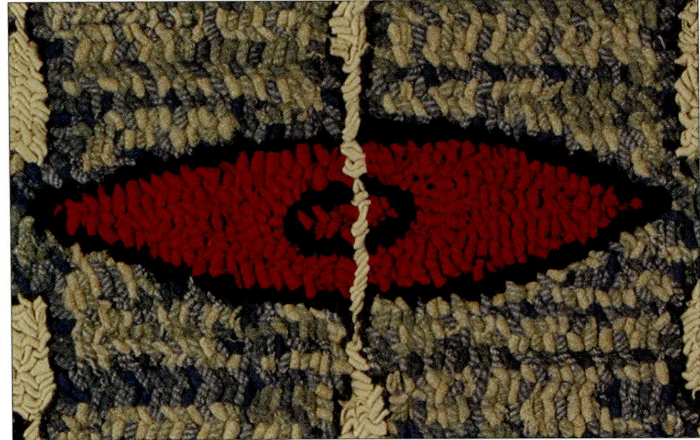

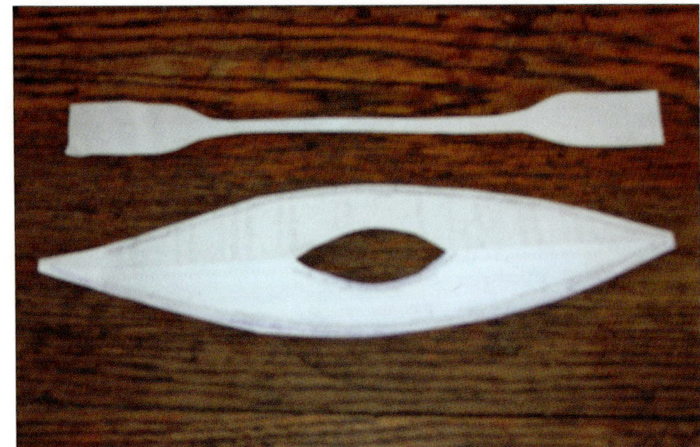

PICTORIAL SCENES

The following rugs depict special events in my life. They are not exact in the way a camera would be, but as a mind files that memory away. They are of special houses, days at the beach, snowshoeing, and country festivals. It is fun to try to depict movement when you are using wide, hand cut, and ripped strips. I love to hide my initials in the smoke of the chimney or in the clouds in the sky.

"Little House," 1996, 15" x 15". This rug was designed for my mother-in-law's favorite rocking chair. I love the dark blue sky, the purple smoke, and the autumn tree. The fuzzy sheep are hooked with raw sheep's wool. It is not spun at all, but twisted and then hooked in. Collection of John and Pamela Blackford, Hopkington, New Hampshire. Photo by P. Blackford ©2009.

"Little House With Two Trees," 2006, 15" x 15." I liked doing the first little house rug so much I decided to make another one. This one had two trees, sheep, and a gray dog. The sky is not as blue and the trees are greener. My initials are in the grey smoke of the house. Collection of Candy Barefoot, Boothbay Harbor, Maine. Photo by S. Stephenson ©2009.

"Heart's Point," 2002, 32" x 17". I especially love the grass in this rug. The green has lots of browns and tans in it. There is also a hint of the ocean to the right. Author's collection.

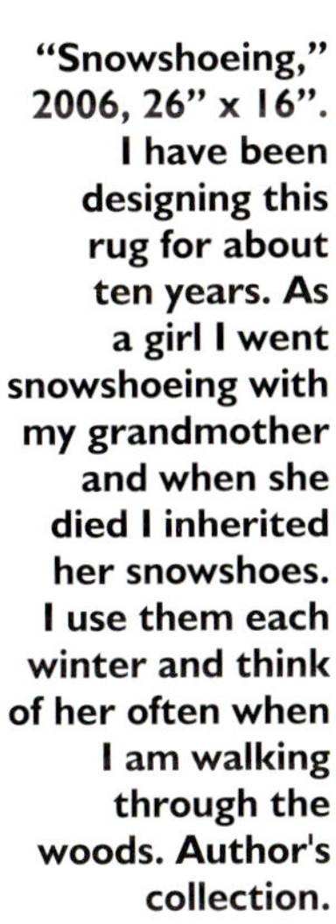

"Snowshoeing," 2006, 26" x 16". I have been designing this rug for about ten years. As a girl I went snowshoeing with my grandmother and when she died I inherited her snowshoes. I use them each winter and think of her often when I am walking through the woods. Author's collection.

"The Skating Party," 2000, 36" x 20". This is my Millennium rug. On New Year's Eve we went to a friend's house for a skating party to welcome in the new century. We skated, fired off muskets and blunderbusts, drank hot chocolate by the fire. We also listened as the coyotes answered the guns with their howls. The ice is an old blanket and the sky swirls were a lot of fun to make. Collection of Charles and Becky Benton, Edgecomb, Maine.

"The Brick House," 2002, 28" x 18". This piece was made for my friend Valencia Schubert. I used a painting her mother had done as a guide. They frequently go to this family home to cut firewood and make maple syrup. Val's mother brought me a bag of old clothes that had belonged to the family to cut up and put into the rug. Her family's initials are around the border and her children's initials are in the lilacs and the trees. This rug is a wonderful memory rug. Collection of Valencia Schubert, Belgrade Lakes, Maine.

"Port Joli Beach," 2002, 38" x 31". When I designed this rug I was in Nova Scotia and going to a hook-in with my mother. I had not brought my hooking with me so she gave me a piece of linen and a marker and I designed this rug. I went to Jan's house with my design, a bag of scraps, and my mother. This beach is my sanctuary, my inspiration, and my healing place. Mermaid Rock Collection, Port Joli, Nova Scotia.

"Pine View Farm, New York," 36" x 48". I drew three different sketches from photos of the farm and the heirloom animals and then picked the best one. It was challenging to get all the buildings and animals in the rug. The farmer has black bushy eyebrows so I hooked them and clipped them so they are longer than the rug and stand out. His loyal Jack Russell Terrier is at his side. My initials and the date are once again in the smoke from the chimneys. Collection of George Carroll Whipple III, Pine View Farm, Carmel, New York. Photo by S. Stephenson ©2009.

"Port Joli, Nova Scotia," 2006, 24" x 36". This small house in Nova Scotia is one of the oldest houses in Port Joli. I put the beach roses on the rug along with the razor clams because we find them on the beach. The border is a Pendleton® shirt. I used one stripe for the inner border and the other one for the outer border. Author's collection.

"Damariscotta Mills," 2005, 28" x 19". Near our home in Maine there is a wonderful swimming hole. It has a bridge nearby and a large old mill building. Generations of people have swum there. When the mill was empty, teenagers dared others to jump off the roof into the water below or out of the open windows. Now they jump off the bridge into the water and if they time it just right the water splashes into a car passing over the bridge. Collection of Wesley and Samantha Adams, Bath, Maine.

"Pownalborough Courthouse," 2006, 25" x 18". Near our home in Maine there are many historic houses. The Pownalborough Courthouse in Dresden is one of the most famous. Thomas Jefferson tried cases there and Martha Ballad, a famous Maine midwife, was asked to testify there many times. Each fall people encamp there while taking part in the many activities of early American life. I hooked this rug after one such October weekend. I used my favorite Woolrich® blue and green shirt for the water and a lighter blue for the sky. Author's collection.

"Home," 2002, 10" x14". This rug was inspired by a house near Shelburne, Nova Scotia. The house is very tiny and the sheep and clouds are hooked with raw wool. In Private Collection. Photo by P. Blackford.© 2009

BELOVED ANIMALS

Most of us have loved a pet, it might be a small kitten, a large dog, or some barnyard fowl. Animals live closely with us and we know them. They console us when we are sad, they play with us, and they sleep with us. Before people had cameras they hooked rugs of their pets to help remember them once they were gone. We hook rugs of our animals for the same reason. Our rugs don't always turn out to look exactly like the pet, but usually they convey the affection we feel. It is challenging to try to get the personality of a pet onto a rug with a few strips of wool. These rugs become family heirlooms because of our connection with these beloved animals.

"Clover", 2006, 12" x 18". This rug was hooked for a little girl whose pet bunny was named Clover. The bunny was hooked with mohair and could be brushed so the pile on the wool stood up and was soft and fluffy. I put in the four leaf clovers in the corners to represent good luck. Collection of Hall Whipple Rockefeller, New York, New York.

"Best Friends," 2007, 18" x 26". I hooked this rug around the same time I hooked the Blue Birds one. If you look at them closely, you can see a lot of similarities. Author's collection.

MAX
Max is our cat. Sometimes
he was one of four tigers in the litter. He was the only one with the white stripe down his nose. The background was great shirts
I changed the border and I really like the wiggly lines, plus the red dots bring all the reds together. Max died Spring 2005 quite unexpectedly and suddenly taking us all by surprise.
SBS MAX 2001
Photos by Nathaniel Blackford age 10

Sketch book page of Max.

"Max," 2001, 28" x 17". Max was one of four tigers in his litter and the only one with a white stripe down his nose. The background was hooked using two fabulous wool shirts which blended nicely without the help of overdyeing. Max died in the spring of 2005, quite unexpectedly. My daughter Maggie told me, "Do not sell the MAX rug. I want it!" I am very pleased to have a record of this special cat. Collection of Maggie Hoyt, Edgecomb, Maine.

Detail of Lucy and the wool roving loosely hooked in and left long.

"Maggie's Cats and the Rainbow," 1997, 38" x 25". This is Maggie's rug. She helped me design it. When I was finished hooking the rainbow I used all the leftover strips and hooked the large border. None of the wool for this rug was dyed at all. I used all leftover pieces in the border, not dyed or married because at that time I was really nervous about dyeing. Collection of Maggie Hoyt, Edgecomb, Maine.

"Fessic," 1996, 31" x 24". I taught for fifteen years. My last job was in the oldest established schoolhouse in Maine. There was a special cat that lived there named Fessic. He would hang out in various classrooms, visiting students and occasionally helping with a lesson. Collection of Edgecomb Eddy Elementary School, Edgecomb, Maine.

"Fish Cat," 2007, 21" x 16". Author's collection. Once, when we lived in Nova Scotia, we had a small, female cat that had belonged to a fisherman. The only thing she would come to was "Fish" because this is what the fisherman would yell when he brought home his catch.

"Red Raven," 2002, 18" x 18". This chair pad was hooked as a Christmas present for a friend. It was bound off in yellow wool, then two pieces of edging were cut like stairs and a single yellow French knot was put in each triangle. Collection of Charles and Becky Benton, Edgecomb, Maine.

"Rooster" chair pad, 1999, 15" x 15". This rooster is very primitive. He has many colors in his tail and body. The antique black in this rug is quite dark. Collection of John and Pamela Blackford, Hopkington, New Hampshire. Photo by P. Blackford ©2009.

"Buddy," 2004, 32" x 17". Buddy's inspiration was a flat-backed cookie cutter. The leafy shapes in the corners are also cookie cutters. The background is a hodgepodge of leftover wool, not married at all. Author's collection.

"The Stag Party," 2007, 30" diameter. I drew a simple little sketch on a piece of paper. I liked making the stags individualized by changing their antlers and I really enjoyed dyeing the browns for the stags, the acorns, and leaves in the center. This rug is only two colors, brown and black. Each one of these colors consists of many different colors. This is what makes it so interesting. Collection of Tom Blackford, Edgecomb, Maine.

"Single Deer," 2003, 15" x 15". I love the simple lines of the deer and the multicolored grey background. The variations of grey remind me of granite rock. That would make this deer a petroglyph. Collection of Betty Bilbrey, Tulsa, Oklahoma. Photo by P. Blackford ©2009.

"Two Autumn Deer," 2003, 38" x 24". This rug has the same colors as "Autumnal Squares." I love the fall colors and the night sky. I can't decide if they look like they are getting ready to mate or to fight. What do you think? Author's collection.

"Lucy in a Sky of Diamonds," 2006, 29" x 17". I really like the way I divided the diamonds up with yellow, not black. It opens the rug up and invites the person looking at it into the rug. Author's collection.

Hugo, also known as, "Black Dog." This was commissioned by a couple for their son. I worked from photographs as the dog was deceased. The date is in the corner and I signed my initials on the dog's hip, hidden unless you look closely. Collection of Prescott McCurdy, Harpswell, Maine.

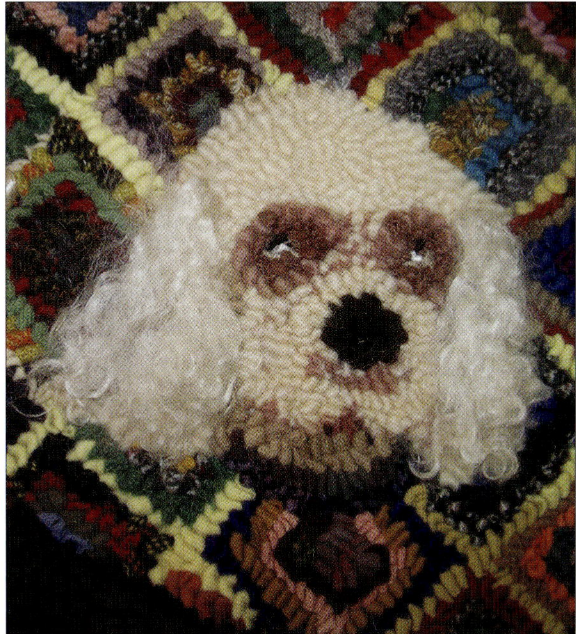

"All the Dogs." This rug was also commissioned by the same couple for their daughter. They wanted all the dogs on it that their daughter had owned. The small dog with the fluffy ears was a challenge. I hooked and sewed in mohair locks and they were dyed with the wool roving in tea to change the color slightly so it wasn't so stark. Collection of Heidi West, Harpswell, Maine.

"Zippy et All," 2006, 16" x 24". Our cat Zippy replaced Max, if any cat can really replace another. She is a Maine coon cat, without the papers. Zippy was hooked out of a Pendleton® shirt. The background is a blanket dyed with onionskins and her kittens have all been hooked out of wools and tweeds that helped me convey their personalities. Collection of Lucy Harrington, Maine.

"Sara Cat," 2007, 13" x 13". This rug was done for a woman named Sara whose cat was a fat and happy tiger. I hid my initials in the background, but put both her name and the date in red so it would show up. The background was dyed with onionskins. The wool for the cat was stained with tea bags before it was hooked. Private Collection.

"Susie Cat," 2001, 13" x 13". I always seem to have a black cat in my life. I put my whole name on this one when I signed it. I put the tulip designs in the corners and the cut zigzagged border (saw toothed) was hand sewn onto the back. Author's collection.

"Sam," 2001, 54" x 38". Sam is a border collie/Australian shepard mix. I like to hook cat rugs and had so many that I decided to hook one of Sam. The hardest part of this rug was getting a photo or sketch of him lying down. Every time I'd look at him, he'd jump up and come to me! This rug hooked up fast because all the strips were already cut and it is basically a geometric. Collection of Sam Stephenson Blackford.

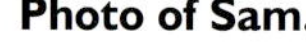

Photo of Sam.

"Ollie," 2004, 26" x 19". Ollie is my sister's dog. He is part border collie. I used a photo to sketch the rug and then hook it. I was pleased with the variations of blue in the background. Collection of Laurie Stephenson and Sue Sirrs, Halifax, Nova Scotia.

This is the pull-toy my father carved for me. I designed a rug for him using this pull toy.

"Papa's Boy," 2002, 20" x 18". When I was a child we had a pony and her colt. We named the colt Papa's Boy Button Brown after both my grandfathers. Collection of Tom Stephenson, Port Joli, Nova Scotia.

"Quaint Folk Art Horse," 2005, 25" x 18". This very happy horse is hooked from my Great Aunt Lizzy's wool pants. The reverse tongues on the border of this rug are all strips of different wool shirts. Author's collection.

"Melody," 2007, 15" x 15". This small mat was made of Button Brown's mother. She was a beautiful pony who would let us ride her but would take us straight to the apple trees in an attempt to scrape us off her back. Collection of Charles and Becky Benton, Edgecomb, Maine.

"In My Dreams," 2006, 40" diameter. Sometimes I dream of wild, impossible animals. One morning I woke up and remembered some of my dreams, quickly got them on paper, and decided to hook it as I had dreamed it, in vivid wild colors. I put a dot in the middle and then hooked the red flower there to center it. In the border, I mirrored the red with the reverse tongues and a black dot in each one. Antique black connects all the animals and symbols. Collection of Jay Stephenson, Reneé Post, and Jack Stephenson, Flourtown, Pennsylvania.

"Blue Birds," 2006, 16" x 24". This rug has two blue birds on it and a heart urn. The birds are very primitive. Their wings are hooked out of a paisley shawl, as is the heart. My initials and the date are hidden under the heart. The background is a blanket dyed with onionskins, plus many other fabrics. Collection of Stephanie Zinger, Shelter Island, New York.

Sketch of "Wild Things."

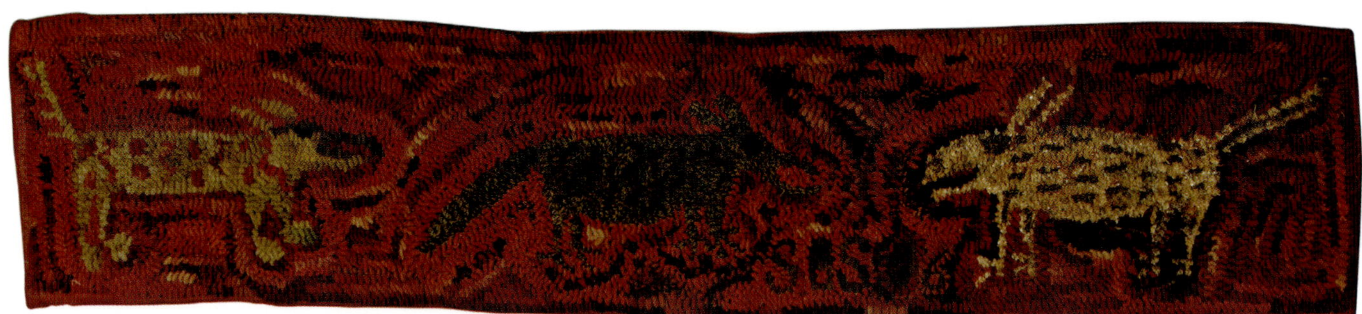

"Wild Things," 2006, 49" x 9". I sketched these wild looking dogs or coyotes, some were fat, others skinny, and striped. This background was dyed reddish brown and it hooked up so fast. It is fun to see how much personality you can portray from pulling up a few loops here and there. Collection of Susan Metters and Mark Segar, Portland, Maine.

Mermaids and Other Nautical Themes

I love mermaids. The idea of them intrigues me; half woman, half fish. I live on the coast and the ocean is very real and powerful to me. Whether on a hot summer's day at the beach, sailing full tilt under a cloudy sky with a storm threatening, or in the dark of winter in a gale with rooster tails coming off the waves. I love the water in all seasons. I also respect it. With that comes thoughts of life under the ocean's surface, we have only just begun to explore it. So, who's to say there really isn't such a thing as mermaids?

My first mermaids were tiny. I used a variety of fabrics, even pantyhose, for the body and wool strips or yarn for the tail. Both body and tail are hooked very high and clipped in the Waldoboro Style. The Waldoboro style is a type of hooking done in and around Waldoboro, Maine. Yarn or wool strips were pulled through the linen very high and close together. Then it was clipped and trimmed to obtain a sculptured appearance. This was done mostly for flowers.

I've done a series of mermaids and fisherman. All the mermaids were hooked high, clipped in the Waldoboro style then decorated with beads, jewelry, pearls, and even my own hair. Backgrounds were painted on the linen and each mat was then placed in an old antique frame.

"Captured Mermaid," 2003, 8" x 9". Artist's collection.

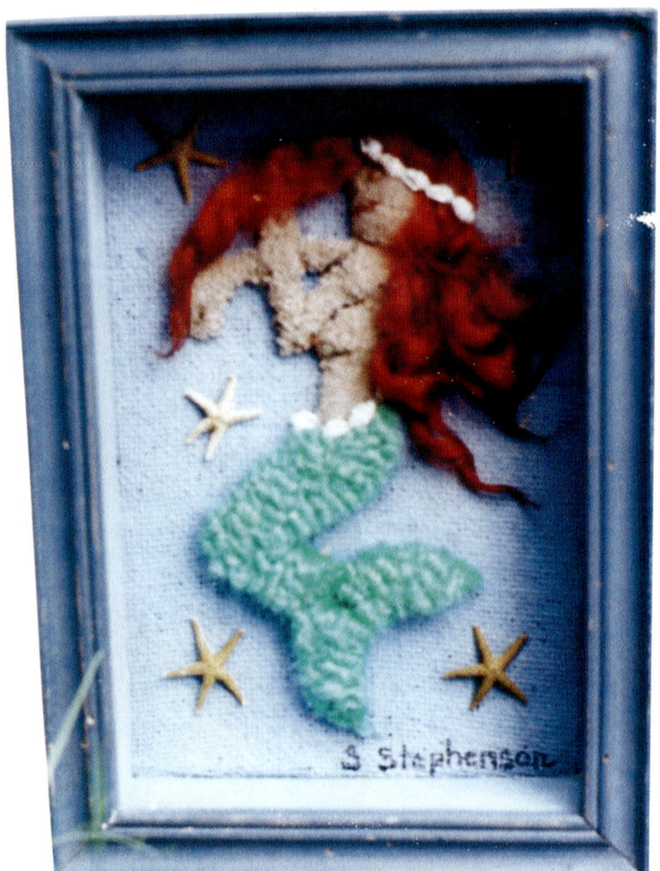

"Captured Mermaid with Red Hair," 2004, 8" x 14". In private collection.

"Captured Mermaid in Shadowbox," 2004, 8" x 14". Artist's collection.

Mermaid Book Cover, 2004, 14" x 10". In private collection.

"Single Mermaid," 2005, 16" x 24". Collection of Laurie Stephenson and Sue Sirrs, Halifax, Nova Scotia.

"Single Mermaid," 2005, 16" x 24". Collection of Laurie Stephenson and Sue Sirrs, Halifax, Nova Scotia.

"Three Mermaids," 2004, 30" x 27". Hooked mermaids on a painted background. Author's collection

"Shipwreck and Mermaids," 2004, 16" x 18".

"The Fisherman and the Mermaids," 2005, 33" x 27". Mermaid Rock Collection, Port Joli, Nova Scotia.

"The Lighthouse Keeper," 2005, 34" x 25". In this rug, the fisherman is rowing home to the lighthouse. His angry wife is waiting, hands on her hips as the mermaids frolic, some alluring, others very voluptuous. Some even pregnant. One of these has some of my own hair in it. Author's collection.

"Mussels and Mermaids" or "Circle of Friends," 2005, 39" diameter. This was the first round rug I attempted. I used two templates. The dozen mermaids on this rug each symbolize a woman, a family member, or friend who is important to me in some way. This rug feels powerful and moving. Even with the pastel shades of greens, blues and tans in it. There is a lot of movement in it, because of the direction of the hooking. Collection of Sandra and Stanley McCurdy, Harpswell, Maine.

"Maine Mermaids," 2006, 36" x 25". These seven mermaids are in squares of light blue sea. They are separated from each other by colors you'd find on the beach. Author's collection.

"The Goddess Within," 2005, 39" x 65". In the spring of 2005 my husband Tom and I went to a very small island in the West Indies called Union Island. I had long extensions braided to my hair and a glorious tan. I felt very attractive for probably the first time in my life. I remember feeling like I was riding on the crest of a wave, like I could attempt anything and it would happen. It was incredible to feel like the universe and I were one. One night I had a dream about walking across a beach with a girlfriend wearing nothing but silk scarves around our middles. The dream seemed to go on forever, with so many symbols, it was absolutely wild. The dream and the idea would not go away. It had to be put onto a rug. As I hooked I wasn't sure how to include all the ideas and symbols of importance from my life and the dream, but I was sure it would come to me. She represents the goddess within us all. She is always there but often covered up, hidden, oppressed. When she awakens and emerges she is unstoppable. I believe she is in us all, just waiting until the time is right to surface. Author's collection.

I HAVE HEARD THE SEA MAIDS' MUSIC
IT IS THE SEA MINGLED WITH THE SUN AND MIST
THEY CALL ME TO JOIN THEM

"Sea Maids' Music," 2007, 56" diameter. My last mermaid rug is a huge one, which, at first glance, looks like there are twelve mermaids swimming to the center swirl. On closer inspection you can see that one of the mermaids is actually a woman swimming among them. Again, each mermaid represents a different woman in my life who is really important to me; my grandmothers, my mother, my daughter, my sisters, and my friends. I wrote my own poem to go around the edge to make it different from my first one. It was tricky lettering all that and keeping it even. I dyed four large batches of blues for this. I divided them all up into four piles and used them all. I think it makes a very interesting background for a rug, when it is hooked with many colors and in varying directions. Author's collection.

"Tom's Boat," 2001, 15" x 15". My husband, Tom, built this boat. I transferred the picture onto the linen and tried to put us in it, wearing our re-enactment clothes. The flag came out really well. I almost ran out of blue for the sky, that's why it consists of so many different blues. I think this makes it look older. Antique rugs quite often have parts that have different colors or a few loops strategically placed so you know they ran out of a color but used something close enough to allow them to finish the rug. The sail was an old blanket dyed with onion skins. Collection of John and Pamela Blackford, Hopkington, New Hampshire. Photo by P. Blackford ©2009.

"Ships at Sea," 2001, 28" x 20". This rug was inspired by a dilapidated cape in Birchtown, Nova Scotia. The actual house was built by freed slaves during the American Revolution. I left a piece of my heart there in Hartz Point the day we found this house. I hand-cut my wool and hooked this rug in a week. The sails are an old cream-colored blanket, the sky was dyed with onion skins and beet juice saved from pickling my beets. The water was a checkered Woolrich® shirt. I put my initials in the smoke coming out of the chimney. The water has a real choppy feel to it. Author's collection.

"Ship in the Pink Sky," 2006, 16" x 24". I love to hook boats and decided to try one with an interesting sky, not blue. The pinks in the sky and water are dyed with beet juice. Are they out for an evening sail or is a storm approaching? Collection of Roberta Schwartz, Topsham, Maine.

"Three Boats," 2006, 30" x 18". I find this shape so pleasing. It reminds me of our boat my husband lofted and built. I hooked the sky with the light strip of a blue and cream blanket. The water was hooked with the dark strip of the same blanket. Author's collection.

"Seduction of the Sea," 2007, 24" x 36". This rug is of a young woman resting against a wood piling. Her hair is blowing in the wind and becoming one with the ocean. The ocean is alive with fanciful creatures. Off in the upper right hand corner is a ship sailing into the waters. Collection of Sandra and Stanley McCurdy, Harpswell, Maine.

WELCOME MATS AND MOTTO RUGS

There is something wonderful about a rug at the door, especially one that is homemade. They do take a lot of abuse by the door, but Welcome mats are made to welcome people into our homes. There is something endearing about a homemade welcome mat, but if they are not put by the door where should they be?

Until I started organizing rugs, photos, and stories for this book I thought I had just done the ones in my scrapbook. I was overwhelmed when I started recording them and putting them into groups and realizing how many I had forgotten that I had hooked.

"Welcome Mat," 1995, 32" x 16". Doesn't this one look old? This was my first Welcome Mat. I drew two hearts, one on each end. I hooked one and then changed the second to a flower. The edge was finished and then the bound petals were added. Author's collection.

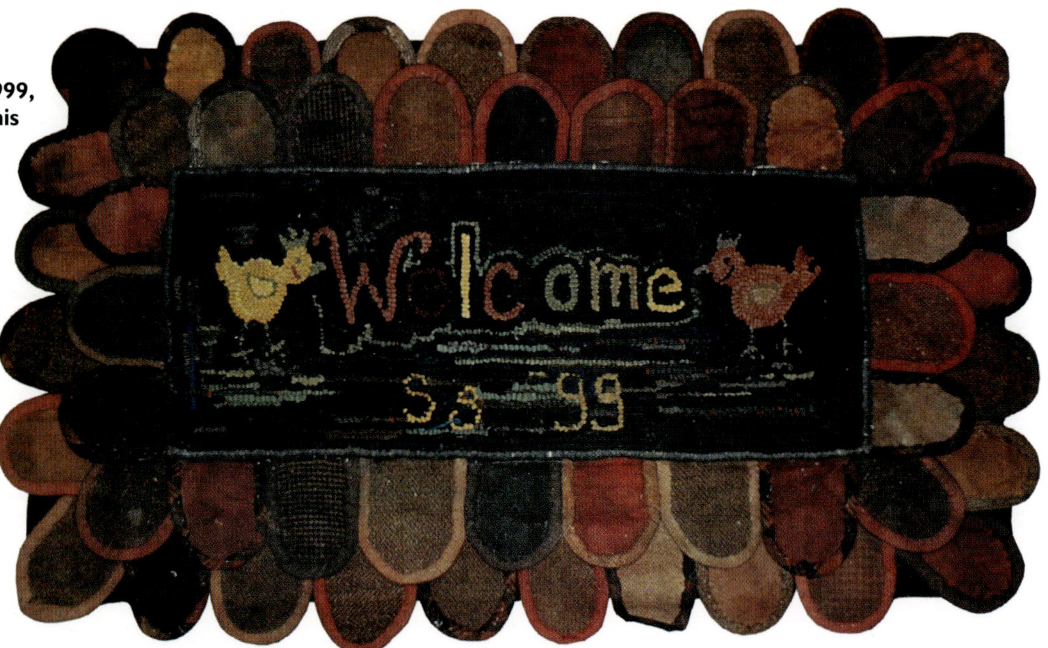

"Welcome Chickens," 1999, 40" x 29". I hooked this welcome mat on a very small piece of linen and then somehow needed to make it big enough to be useful. I cut out the tongues or petals and edged them with wool cut on the bias so it stretched. I sewed them all and when my mom came to visit we dyed them. We got to talking and left them in the dye pot too long. I think the colors married quite well. Author's collection.

"Welcome Chickens in Brown and Green," 2004, 36" x 16". One more variation on the same theme, chickens, welcome, and petals. I dyed these in my iron pot over my fireplace to marry them. I pulled it off the fire and put it on the doorstep to cool. We didn't use that door much, and it sat there for three days, freezing and thawing, before I remembered it. I think that's what made it look so old. Collection of Tom and Joan Stephenson, Port Joli, Nova Scotia.

"Blue Welcome Mat," 2005, 36" x 17". ,This welcome mat has off-white chickens, a background of a blue Pendleton® shirt and the word "welcome" hooked in various colors. The chickens appear to be all white, but on closer inspection you can see that the wings are hooked of grey, green, and tan strips. The tongues were all the same; grey wool with an edge of navy blue cut on the bias. This is so boring to sew, but when the rug is finished the simple color scheme is very pleasing. Author's collection.

"Two Crows Joy," 2008, 26" x 16". I wanted to hook a rug with this whole saying on it. It is called Counting Crows. I did some research on it and found that it is English. We said it in Maine when I was little and then in Nova Scotia too. There are so many variations of it, I was left unsure of the one I wanted to place on my rug and hook, so I just put "Two Crows Joy" and hooked that with a red background. Author's collection.

"Simple Things Hold Secrets," 2005, 33" x 14". This motto rug has a saying on it that I truly believe. Simple things are special and they do hold secrets. Just look at old folk art. Author's collection

"Enough is an Abundance," 2003, 40" x 29". Author's collection.

"Less is More," 2002, 38" x 19". This is another one of my family's favorite sayings, although none of us follow it! It is hooked with a nice, soft mustard background and four red padullas in the corner. They are outlined in the same blue as the saying and the border ties it all together. There is a lot of movement in this piece with the S's and other swirls in the background. Author's collection.

"Enough is an Abundance," 1996, 29" x 19". I wish I followed this motto every day! The petals are three layers of wool, stitched to each other before being sewn to the actual rug. The actual rug backing is burlap and the edges were just turned under before the tongues were attached. A thin piece of wool was sewn over the edges of the tongues and the edges of the rug to neaten up the back. Collection of Tom and Joan Stephenson, Port Joli, Nova Scotia.

PADULLAS AND OTHER FLOWERS

Padullas are flowers that don't really look like any particular flower. It is a vague term used in rug hooking for an old flower. They can be any shape or color to fit into your color scheme. I like Padullas in rugs, they are charming, childlike, and friendly.

"Padullas and Reverse Tongues," 2000, 32" x 20". My mother hooked this rug with a dark green background and I loved it so much I tried to make one like it. We like to sit in the comfortable chairs with a roaring fire in the fireplace and hook and visit. I traced the petal with paper and I was ready. It was a very simple rug to hook. I just drew the flower on and tried to make a leaf. When I made the triangles I kind of fudged them so they'd fit between the edges. Author's collection.

"Dark Medallion or Padulla," 2003, 38" x 21". A few years later I decided to do another rug, roughly the same. I enlarged the flower so it kind of looks like a medallion. It is fun to see the same pattern interpreted in different ways with different colors. Artist's Collection.

"Loud's Island Mallow," 2001, 13" x 13". This plant grows wild and abundant on Loud's Island. The clouds are hooked with raw sheep's wool, pulled loosely so it stands out a bit from the background. In private collection.

"Purple Morning Glories," 2003, 31" x17". Mermaid Rock Collection, Port Joli, Nova Scotia.

"Red Padullas with Green Background," 2008, 33" x 24". One day I was wandering around an antique shop and came across an interesting iron form. It was too expensive for me to buy, but I sketched the form in my notebook. The background is two blazers married with some blues. The poison is this rug is the four yellows in the centers. Author's collection.

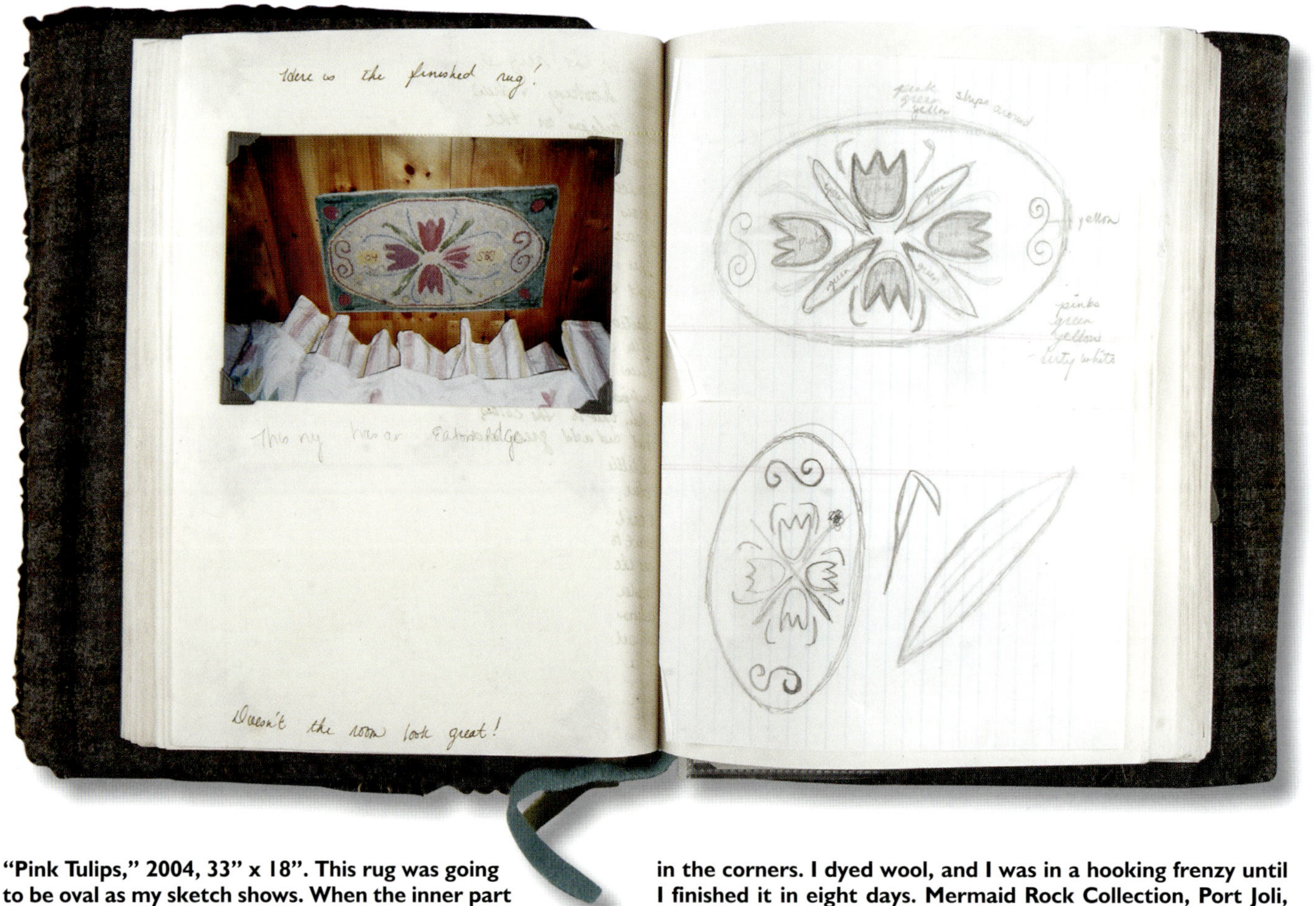

"Pink Tulips," 2004, 33" x 18". This rug was going to be oval as my sketch shows. When the inner part was done it just didn't look right so I hooked it to the end of the linen and made the outer part green with pink buds in the corners. I dyed wool, and I was in a hooking frenzy until I finished it in eight days. Mermaid Rock Collection, Port Joli, Nova Scotia.

GEOMETRICS

Geometrics are perhaps one of the easiest rugs to hook. They use up a lot of left over wool scraps from other projects and there is a freedom about hooking them that I love. There is a lot of planning in the beginning. I suggest doing this when you are alone and can actually think clearly. You might want to make a few notes. Geometrics are a simple form repeated over and over to form a design. Small or large circles, squares, lines, templates, cups and saucers can all be used.

Graph paper is helpful when sketching a design, mostly because you want to have enough space to complete your design and know how many repetitions you will need to make it look pleasing. Usually an uneven number is more pleasing to the eye than an even amount.

For planning out a geometric, I suggest using a long yard stick, a tape measure, and whatever template you desire. You also need a sharp pencil and a permanent black Sharpie® marker. Because they have no up and down, they look right from any direction.

"Log Cabin Design," 1996, 26" x 30". This rug is an old design. It was fun and fast to hook because all my strips were cut and I used up the leftover colors from other rugs. This rug is still very bright even after being used for twelve years. Collection of John and Pamela Blackford, Hopkington, New Hampshire. Photo by S. Stephenson ©2009.

"Simple Stripes," 1995, 27" x 20". Stripes are probably the easiest geometric to do. They are simple to design, easy to hook, and useful. I used up lots of my sewing scraps and strips my mother gave me to hook this piece.

"Large Hit and Miss with Four Padullas," 1994, 36" x 32". This piece of burlap was old and the edge was all bound off with black cotton cloth turned twice. I drew lines to make squares and then filled in each with strips of different colors. Near the end of this one, I was so bored with the straight lines that I drew a large flower in each corner and hooked it in pink using part of an old sweater. This rug really looks like an antique. Author's collection.

"Compass Rose," 1995, 16" diameter. This small compass rose was drawn with a large boat builder's compass and each section was hooked with a stripe from an old wool blanket. The colors blend in so nicely. Collection of Art and Dawn Garey in Edgecomb, Maine. Photo by P. Blackford ©2009.

"Cat's Paw," 1995, 24" x 15". This is a very old pattern. I hooked this one in the fall. Be careful you don't hook circles so tightly that they dome up. Author's collection.

"Black and Grey Medallion (Broiler)," 2004, 64" x 28". This iron boiler was seen in an antique shop in Maine. I got a large piece of linen and traced the design on, going in three ways. The grey is actually many different colors and textures. The background is hooked in straight lines that hook up very quickly. It is dark, yet comforting. Author's collection.

"Shamrock," 1999, 15" x 15". This shamrock was made up of four simple hearts. A star was placed in the middle of each one. Collection of John and Pamela Blackford, Hopkington, New Hampshire.

"Cream and Blue Geometric Star," 2007, 13" x 13". When I was small, I remember my mother and my Aunt Ruth sitting at the table, drinking coffee, smoking cigarettes, and talking. My Aunt Ruth would draw these intricate designs with her ballpoint pen on any scrap of paper available. When I hooked this small mat I had to simplify it a lot to make it fit onto the linen or else it would have turned into a huge rug. My Aunt Ruth hooked also. She did not design her own rugs, but hooked other people's designs. I often think of her and what her mats would have looked like if she had designed her own. I'm sure they would have been breathtaking. Author's collection.

"Brown and Blue Waves," 2007, 17" x 15". One day I was thinking about wavy lines painted on some furniture and I decided to play around with the idea. It is fun to see how many different colors one can use in a two-tone rug and still have it appear to be two colors. Author's collection.

"Autumnal Squares," 2004, 18" x 24". This rug was hooked using the leftover pieces of the two deer rugs. I had cut way too much wool. Collection of Rosa Brugnoni, Umbertide, Umbria, Italy.

“33 “Swirls,” 2006, 21” x 16”. This rug was all those swirls of different vibrant colors that most of us never put into a rug. I loved using all these crazy colors, then added a black background and called it good. Author's collection.

“Autumn Squares and Squiggles,” 2007, 54” x 31”. Each square is eight inches by eight inches. I outlined each square with an old army blanket. I also used this to hook the squiggly line from corner to corner. Then I followed the contours of the squiggly line. In one corner instead of doing the squiggly line I put my name, Susie, and hooked around that. The date is hidden there, too. Author's collection.

HOOKED ITEMS OTHER THAN RUGS

People ask me all the time about what I do. I decided to make some items to take with me so that when I am asked I can get these out to show people. All of them are great conversation starters. People are very interested in the technique of hooking.

Sunflowers and pumpkin pins, 2000-2008, 2-3 inches. There are many varieties of pins to make. I enjoy making them to suit the season and have one to wear on my sweater, blazer, or coat. They also make nice small gifts.

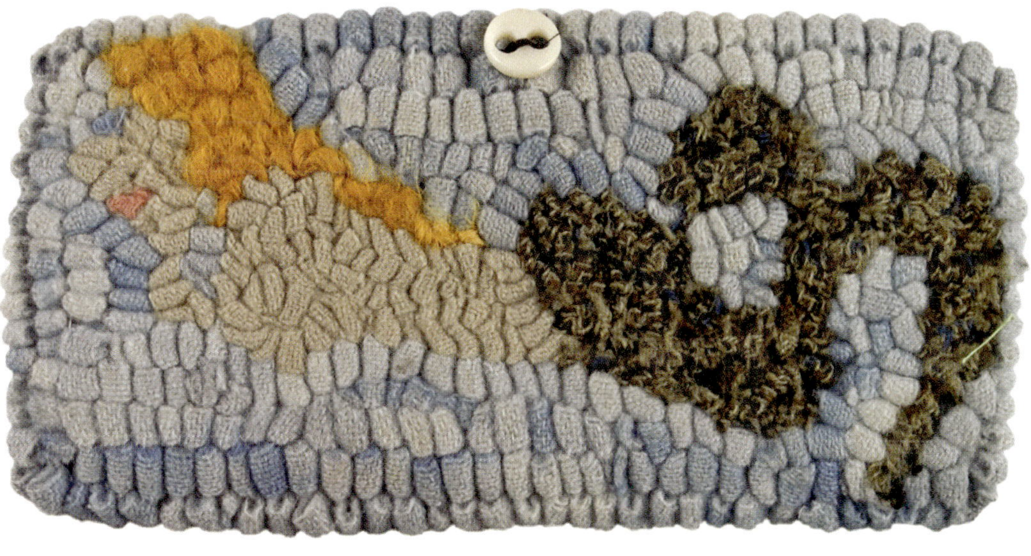

My purchased wallets never stay together. So I decided to make one, then a few more.

Cardholder, inside and out.

A few bags, big and small.

Mermaid bags.

A book cover.

Santa decorations, filled with balsam.

Hat and shoes.

Hat, mittens, gloves and shoes

Hooked bikini, 2008, small. What do you wear for swimming in the cold Maine waters? A wool bikini! Someone looked at me once when I was wearing my coat and shoes and asked, "Is your underwear hooked too?" At that time it was not, but now I can confidently say with a little smirk on my face, "Yes!" Artist's collection.

"Hooked Padulla Vest," 2007. My vest was hooked in one piece. The fall colors are comforting. It is a delight to wear my vest and I'm sure it will be for you to wear yours. People are always stopping and asking me questions about it. It is more versatile than my coat because I can wear it more often throughout the year and I can wear it inside too! This vest is an interesting conversation piece and is not something you can buy off the rack. People know this and respond to it. They also love it when I show them the lining.

Label of "Hooked Padulla Vest."

Vest before sewing.